"Everyday people, people like you and me, have discovered that devastating challenges can be faced when faith, hope, and love are the focal points of a Jesus-kind of life."

This book is a work of Bible Study and encouragement. The names have been changed to provide anonymity to those involved, but the stories related by the author are true and actual events. The New International Version of the Bible was used for all quotes unless otherwise noted.

All right reserved. No part of this book may be used or reproduced by any means, graphic, electronic, or mechanical including photocopying, recording, taping or by any information storage retrieval system without the written permission of author except in the case of brief quotations embodied in critical articles and reviews.

Scripture taken from the Holy Bible, New International Version, Copyright 1973, 1978, 1984, by International Bible Society. Used by permission of Zondervan. All rights reserved.

Because of the dynamic nature of the Internet, any web addresses or links contained in this book may have changed since publication and may no longer be valid. Views are those of the author.

"Everyday Jesus for the Everyday Life" is (c) 2018 by Randy Whitehead. All rights reserved. Contact through e-mail randallwwhitehead@yahoo.com.
ISBN-13: 9781987596465
ISBN-10: 1987596463

Everyday Jesus for the Everyday Life

by

Randy Whitehead

Index

Introduction: Learning to Live Without the Miracles -- 7

    1. *Dealing with Your Prisons -- 13*

    2. *Not Even His Brothers Believed Him --21*

    3. *A Close and Lasting Relationship --29*

    4. *Giving Back to Caesar --38*

    5. *Finding Joy at Work --48*

    6. *Oodles of Noodles --57*

    7. *When Thorns Take Over Your Bed of Roses --65*

    8. *Sometimes I Forget That --73*

    9. *You Talked My Leg Off --82*

    10. *The Unexpected Expected --91*

Conclusion: Making an Everyday Jesus Live
                Everyday in Our Lives --100

> *An Everyday Jesus for the Everyday Life – Introduction*
> # Learning to Live Without the Miracle
> *"Understanding Jesus' Plan"*

Suzanna saw them first. Her gasp brought her identical twin friends Terri and Mary to the open back door. The four of us were shutting down the restaurant for the night but the sight outside demanded an audience. These three very intelligent and impressionable young ladies had never before seen what we call the aurora borealis or the "Northern Lights". In fact, only cold nights like this one teased the glimmering flickers into our part of southeastern Illinois.

If you have never seen the Northern Lights, you would identify them as beautiful in an eerie sort of way. The Northern Lights are the result of sub-atomic particles being blown free of the sun. Some of those particles manage to enter the atmosphere of the earth over the North or South Pole where the protective atmosphere of the earth is somewhat weaker. Those particles then collide with volatile gases some 60 miles above the earth at the poles creating minute explosions of light that brilliantly dance through the sky. Usually the lights are either green or pink in color based on the kind of gas the particles bombard. Other colors are possible, however, if different gases are present where the bombardment takes place. One story says that if the observer whistles, the lights will flicker even brighter. I have never been able to prove it. [1]

The usually talkative young ladies were unusually quiet. Suzanna walked back from the door with Mary and Terri in tow. Her lips began to quiver, and a strange pallor covered her face. With fear hiding behind her voice, her question was straightforward and simple, "Randy, is it the end of the world?" She had never seen such a sight. The mechanics of God's handiwork in the northern sky had attracted her attention. It caused her to think about what she had never thought about before—there is something out there bigger than she, that is controlled by someone mightier than she, that she must find a way to deal with. God's miracles always seem to have that effect.

I assured all three young ladies that this was not the end of the world. That night we discussed how the world would end and how Christ would come. Once again, a great miracle of God moved in the hearts of everyday people.

God often used miracles to attract attention to Himself. During Noah's adventure, God put a rainbow in the sky to promise He would never again destroy the world by flood. The Israelites were amazed at God's provision when the Red Sea parted and when the Jordan river became a land bridge for the feet of God's people. A boy's lunch of five loaves of bread and two small fish became the buffet for more than 5000 men and whomever else happened to be there.

But while miracles have played an important role in introducing God's Son to the hearts of everyday men, some of the most significantly changed lives have come from simply meeting Jesus and discovering the hope and strength in the life lessons He teaches. Many everyday people, people just like you and me, have discovered that life can be exhilarating and filled with purpose when we learn and practice the principles that Jesus taught. Everyday people, people like you and me, have discovered that devastating challenges can be faced when faith, hope, and love are the focal points of a Jesus-kind of life. Moreover, everyday people, people just like you and me, faced death by Rome's lions and on pitch-covered burning crosses because the message of the Savior carried them bravely through every trial. There was something in the man Jesus and His teachings they could not explain, something that made life purposeful and even victorious!

To see how this is true, let us look at some of Jesus' contemporaries. After all, they saw Him with their own eyes. They heard Him with their own ears. They would be the ones who would know if Jesus was a fake or the real thing!

Let's meet Zacchaeus. Luke 19 gives us his story. Jesus was passing through the area of Jericho, a city with a rich history, worthy of your study. In this story, we learn three things about Zacchaeus. First, he was wealthy. Secondly, he was a chief tax collector. Thirdly, he was short!

He was wealthy because he was a chief tax collector. Rome used local people to collect taxes and oversee the tax policies it mandated. It was the job of "chief" tax collectors to organize the tax collecting process. Rome did not really care about how the money was collected. The government did feel, however, that the provinces should pay their own way so taxes were levied. A tax collector could simply walk up to someone and demand a tax be paid. It is believed that in this province there was a 1% wage tax, crop taxes which included 10% of the grain and 20% of the grape/wine harvest, a sales tax, an emergency tax, and the list goes on. Is it a wonder people did not like tax collectors? And they really did not like chief tax collectors who were figured in with the prostitutes and the worst kind of sinners.[2]

Back to Zacchaeus! We now have this chief tax collector, considered part of the worst of Jewish society, who wants to see Jesus. He is forced to climb up in a tree to do so. Jesus had to be attracting quite a crowd.

Stopping just under the tree, Jesus looks up, I suppose intrigued by sandaled feet, hanging down off the tree branch. Looking further, he sees the sandaled feet are attached to a small body sitting uncomfortably on that branch. Jesus knows it is Zacchaeus. The Savior calls him down and Zacchaeus quickly obeys. The Son of God ignores the muttering of the crowd; Zacchaeus revels in the call of Jesus. The Messiah invites Himself to Zacchaeus' house! The short little despised guy is thrilled.

But there is one more surprise from Zacchaeus. Luke 19:8 says, "But Zacchaeus stood up. He said, 'Look, Lord! Here and now I give half of what I own to those who are poor. And if I have cheated anybody out of anything, I will pay it back. I will pay back four times the amount I took.'" (NIrV) This just wasn't what happened in the life of tax collectors, notorious for extortion and deceit.

This revelation led Jesus to say that salvation had come to Zacchaeus. This was a big change in the life of a little man.

But what caused it? Was it lightening from heaven? Did a wall of waters part? No, it was neither! It was the touch of the everyday Jesus showing compassion and love to the everyday man, a person not unlike you and me.

Jesus has another connection with an everyday person in John 4. This time a woman is in the conversation. This is unique because men did not talk to women in public in that day. And this is also unique because Jews did not talk to Samaritans; they were bitter enemies. Already Jesus is breaking the rules of the day to touch this everyday woman's life.

If you will read through John 4 you will see that they discuss the number of marriages the woman has had. They argue about the place of worship. They also debate the importance of the Messiah and Jesus' revelation to her.

Do you find it odd that NOBODY ever told Jesus He should not be talking to this woman now? Do you find anything strange in the woman's testimony found in John 4:29: "Come. See a man who told me everything I've ever done. Could this be the Christ?" (NIrV)

Once again there is no miracle here. Oh, I suppose we could argue about how Jesus knew about the marriages, but there is also some thought that she was a well-known figure and her life was an open book in the area. But notice there was no bloody river, no flies, no darkness, just the teaching and magnetism of this man Jesus. The everyday Jesus who helped the everyday woman get her life back on track.

We could certainly find some other examples, but these two should be enough to help us see that Jesus could touch the lives of people just by being Jesus, just by loving and caring and sharing in the lives of people, people just like you and me.

You can be assured of one thing, when Jesus did a miracle, there was a great teaching or a great lesson hiding behind the miracle. What would happen if we became less concerned about seeking a miracle and began to look for the life lessons in the teaching of Jesus? What if the healing was not the most important thing in the story of the paralytic let down through the roof? What lesson could we learn from Jesus' teaching about the faith needed to live the Christian life? What new insight could we gain about the kind of love that changes people?

During our reading let us try to see if we can find answers from an everyday Jesus for our everyday lives. We may encounter some miracles along the way, but there is something lurking in these true-to-life stories that will help us survive difficult times even when miracles don't show up as hoped. As we consider the everyday problems we face, my guess is that we can successfully live without miracles. If you are game to try it, join me as we walk together to discover an everyday Jesus for our everyday lives and see what we can learn when miracles are not the answer!

> *An Everyday Jesus for the Everyday Life – Chapter 1*
> **Dealing with Your Prison**
> *"When Fear Imprisons Us"*

Fear is a prison that comes in many shapes and sizes. Incarcerating fear might happen when it seems that a special loved one could walk away. Imprisoning fear for some comes in the shape of losing their livelihood or their lifestyle or even their identity which is closely tied to that job they have had for many years. Fear isolates the senior citizen who feels useless and the child who wonders if that new school really will be such a good idea.

I found myself in prison one day. It happened so fast I didn't see it coming. And there was absolutely no one who could help me get out.

A few years ago, while traveling and doing curriculum training for a major Christian publisher, a three-day trip led me into an unexpected new prison. The two days of trainings and two nights in local hotels were taking their toll on a tired brain and an achy body. These circumstances helped fear rear its ugly head.

Upon leaving Cape Girardeau, Missouri, I chose a route home to avoid the interstate highways and, instead, travel through the beautiful, rolling Southern Illinois countryside. Coming to the edge of town, my prison loomed over me. Ahead of me was the Mississippi River crossing that the local people called the "Old River Bridge". The rusty old bridge brought me to a panic. My terrified foot refused to push the accelerator pedal to head toward the bridge. I was forced to retreat from the bridge entrance and took refuge in the parking lot of an empty gas station trying to figure how to break out.

Upon examination from a safe distance, I scanned my new prison. The top of the bridge, by my reckoning, had to be 150 feet off the water and the deck at least 60 feet off the water, a height necessary for boats to travel the massive river running underneath. The imposing structure, about 25 yards shy of a mile long, was made of unkempt steel. The slender onramp to the two-lane highway bridge added claustrophobia to my fears. The massive steel supports, the iron work over head, and the holes in the pavement revealing the river below did nothing to quiet my shaking nerves or stop the nervous sweating.

What could I do? Sitting in the deserted parking lot, I trembled and cried and prayed. I needed to go home, but there were no ruby slippers to tap together to take me there. While Dorothy made getting to Kansas so simple when she clicked her heels in the Wizard of Oz, there was no such magic waiting for me.

Fear is a strong prison and one Satan can use quite well to keep us off guard. Its affects range from minor distraction to solitary confinement. It eats at us every day, day in and day out, when it has its hold on us. And, quite honestly, fear may well be the underlying problem in all the different life events we will look at throughout this book.

Some years before, in an early ministry, I met a fellow prisoner. The visit we had was the result of one of my church families telling me about the needs of a loved one. He had been in an Evansville, Indiana hospital for several days but he simply was not getting any better. The doctors did not know what to do. The family implored me to go and visit with him. I am confident they believed that I might perform a miracle.

I went trusting God but uncertain about a plan to follow. The hospital room reminded me of buzzards circling a dead carcass. Everyone was standing around, awkwardly trying to find the magic formula that would bring their loved one home. We chatted introductions and then I asked the family if the patient and I could have some time alone. The family members left with looks of sadness, almost hopelessness, in their eyes.

The conversation pivoted around one question. "What's the matter?" And I will never forget his despairing cry, "I'm going to die! I'm going to die!" He was so focused on his illness and its possible outcome that he could not see any hope. He was so afraid he was going to die that he was not able to see how to live. We talked a bit more, prayed together, redirected our focus on Christ, and faced the reality that death will come, but it did not have to come today. I left uncertain about what help I had been.

Two days later the family told me that the man was getting out of the hospital the next day. They did not know what I "did", but their loved one was able to get back to living. The only comment that could be made was that fear is a terrible prison.

This is an important point here, a vital point! What I am going to share in this chapter, and in this book, is not a medical prescription for every ailment known to man. You might need therapy, or you might need a doctor. I don't have a medical certificate or license and I am not state certified to treat all of your needs. If you need a doctor, see a doctor. Get the help you need. But if by refocusing on the teachings of Jesus you can step back into the path that helps your heavenly walk, the difference will be undeniable.

Matthew 14:22-33 talks about a time that Jesus' disciples sailed into prison. They had all just seen a rather remarkable thing when Jesus took five small loaves of bread and two small fish, a boy's lunch, and by the power of God stretched it to feed 5000 men and also women and children who might have been there. Why the disciples are shepherded off so quickly is a bit puzzling until you read John's gospel and see that the crowd was ready to take Jesus by force and make Him king. Jesus was kind enough to keep his disciples out of that storm by moving them into a different kind of storm.

While Jesus was enjoying His solitude and conversation with the Father, well into the night, the disciples faced other issues. Fear was mounting. The prison walls were starting to build. The boat Jesus had put them in was now sailing into the wind. It was being tossed about against the swell that was coming up. These men were experienced sailors and this was a larger boat crossing the sea, as explained by the Greek word used here. The sailors should have been in their element. But they weren't. The Sea of Galilee should have been second nature to them, but this time it did not work that way.

The sea of Galilee is about 13 miles long and a bit over 8 miles wide. A short 33 miles hike would walk you around the Sea. Its deepest depth is thought to be 141 feet. At an altitude of about 700 feet below sea level it is the lowest freshwater lake on the earth. Storm winds are produced as the wind blows down from the West and Northwest into the basin where the Sea lies. The Sea can be quite peaceful and calm. However, when the winds hit, it can be a most dangerous place to maneuver.[3] These disciples were tasting dangers they had not encountered before.

Roll forward a few hours. It is now early in the morning. Jesus has finished His prayers. The disciples are continuing their struggles against the wind.

The Bible doesn't say what prompted Jesus to do what He did next. His disciples were simply thankful that He did. Jesus comes walking to them on the water!

It must have been a terrifying sight. The disciples are fighting for their lives in the boat, wondering about the tomorrow they might never see. A man comes walking on the wind-capped sea. They could hardly believe their eyes. It is then they hear the cry of Matthew 14:27, *"At once, Jesus said to them, 'Don't worry! I am Jesus. Don't be afraid.'"*

Peter, impetuous Peter, recognizing the voice, decides he has to walk on the water. He must be sure. Peter's statement is something like this, "Lord, if it is you, then let me come walking on the water to you!" And Jesus does what any good teacher would do by encouraging Peter to "come on!"

Peter steps out on the water. In excitement he strides out of the boat and impossibly across the water. He is going on a leisurely walk in the midst of the storms that are around him.

And he does GREAT! That is until. . .well, let's let Matthew 14:30 tell the story. *"But when Peter saw how strong the wind was, he was afraid and started sinking. 'Save me, Lord!' he shouted."* Did you notice what it was that caused Peter to look away? He saw how strong the wind was. He started focusing on something other than Jesus. He became afraid and began to sink into the turmoil of the Sea of Galilee.

Jesus is now forced to put his hand out to Peter, pulling him up out of the water. Together they got back into the boat. And, surprisingly, as fast as the storm came up, it stopped.

I have often wondered how Peter felt after that experience. I don't know that there is any follow up to this in the scripture. But I do know the powerful affect it had on the rest of the sailors as the scripture says the men in the boat worshipped Him and identified Jesus as the Son of God.

In the introduction, I noted that there might be some miracles along the way that just jump into view. But I also noted that there is something behind the miracles, some lesson that needs to be learned. If you would be so kind as to indulge me, I think there are three lessons from this scripture that can help us when we are facing the prison of fear, when the miracle doesn't come.

I chose the CEV translation because I really like the way it pulls the first lesson out. That lesson is "Don't worry, *I am Jesus. Don't be afraid!*" (Italics mine)

I recently had a medical situation where I needed to see a specialist. My family doctor suggested one specialist that I did not know; I knew of another doctor in that specialty that I had great faith in. I chose the one I felt was the best based on what I knew and what I could understand.

If you are in personal peril, don't you want the best person you know to save you? I am convinced that is Jesus in life's serious challenges. If I hear the soothing voice of Jesus, or at least the soothing call of Jesus, what could be better than that? I know that Jesus can handle the worst of things so why doesn't it follow that he can handle the small things, eternally speaking of course.

If I am facing a crisis then, I want to hear the voice of someone who can make a difference. Confidently, I trust Jesus! I hope you will too.

If you think back to the story I told about the man in the hospital, you might remember I pointed to one thing that we did together that seemed to help him. We took time to learn lesson number 2. We refocused on Jesus.

A lot of times when we are in fearful situations, we lose our focus. The fear becomes so big, so giant-sized, so encompassing that what we should do we don't think about. If I have a bill that needs to be paid and I don't have the money, my typical action is to worry and fret and stew about not having the money. And it becomes gripping. I may even become sick with worry because the lack of funds is all I can think about.

If we can refocus when a fear situation comes our way, if we can turn our hearts and minds back to Jesus, we often find He has a plan we never thought about. Or if there is no ready answer, at least we remember the one who makes the difference in our lives. That goes a long way toward helping us face the situation head on instead of sticking our heads in the sand.

When my children were young, back in 19???, I was having some anxiety issues about the ministry I was involved in. A Christian counselor had come into our area in a new ministry and it seemed the ideal time to seek some help. As the counselor and I discussed the situations I was facing, he asked me a pointed question, "Have you praised God for this situation?" I had to honestly answer no. Praising God was the farthest thing from my mind! I took his advice and began to praise God for the trouble and His mighty hand already at work. It changed me!

The disciples saw what Jesus had done. They praised Him and realized that He truly was God's Son. It made a change in their lives that they could never have imagined. Praise was so pivotal, it was a focal point of what happened in this story. And it is a necessary lesson 3 for each of us to take home when fear has us imprisoned

Back to the deserted gas station parking lot in Cape Girardeau, Missouri. I'm still setting there. The new bridge was not built for 5 years yet. The fear of the "Old River Bridge" was still my prison. The metal was still 150 feet over the river. The bridge deck was still 60 feet above the water. The pavement still had holes that showed the river below.

It was then I realized that I had to deal with this issue. I could sit no longer. I had to go home. Taking another route was not an option.

The Lord helped me see, like Peter, that I needed to focus on the other side. And just as the men in the boat understood, Jesus was the one who was with me. So carefully, I focused straight ahead, not looking over the sides, not looking at the water below, ignoring the holes in the road under me. In a matter of moments, that 4,744 feet passed under my car and I came to the grade off the bridge onto the Illinois side. I breathed a sigh of relief and uttered a prayer of thanksgiving and praise. And somewhere along the way, I sang to the Audience of One, "My God is an Awesome God!

> *An Everyday Jesus for the Everyday Life – Chapter 2*
> # Not Even His Brothers Believed Him
> *"When Family Disappoints Us"*

It was fun to grow up in my family. Sure, we fought like cats and dogs. But three boys, one girl, and one mom and dad could have all kinds of adventures together.

In our younger days, dad would strap on his guitar and take us to American Legion meetings, church programs, or school activities where we did a VonTrapp Family kind of program (Well, maybe not as adorable, but just as meaningful.) We drove to see grandparents, on both sides of the family, in our old yellow Nash. Lessons to teach us children about farming on the family farm were mostly less than successful (remembering a fence post I destroyed with the combine I was pulling) but they worked and brought us together.

I still remember, as a family, visiting the state capital, sharing our first root beer and hot dogs from an honest to goodness root beer stand, and making a trip to Gettysburg, Pennsylvania. Mom and dad survived the trip and my brothers and sister and I did too!

I would like to think that my wife and I transferred that kind of experience on to our daughters. During a trip to Disney World in Orlando, Florida I vividly remember huddling together in a walk-through restaurant when a severe lightning storm started. Traveling to Denver, Colorado for a church convention was made memorable when our younger daughter got pink eye the first morning there. Riding bikes, visiting family, and making "like-family" out of near-by neighbors became the superglue moments that pulled us together.

And yes, we did fight like cats and dogs and, yes, we did disagree. But my wife and I do have 12 grandkids at this writing and we have discovered that it is true that grandkids are your reward for not killing your kids when they were little.

There were times though that I felt let down by my family. Early one Sunday morning we got a phone call that our younger daughter had been involved in a traffic accident on a dark country road not far from the town where we lived. Getting dressed as quickly as possible, and still not being sure that everything was fastened and zippered as it was supposed to be, I hurried out to the site of the wreck. The car lay on its top with shattered back glass showing the only escape route available. Upon learning the whole story, I was not happy because another person who should not have been driving, had been behind the wheel. But I was so thrilled my daughter was safe. A trip to the emergency room showed she was all right. I could breathe and put things into perspective with love.

Our other daughter let us know that she was not finishing college. I felt let down, but now I realize that was not my decision to make. I wish she could have worked it all out and went through college, although now I understand her decision. And I realize that both she and our younger daughter have become wonderful Christian women in their own right. I guess I would not change anything for the world. You may also know the joy of a wonderful family. You might be the best friend to your son or daughter. You might help watch your grandchildren and even get them off to school. Perhaps you look at their diplomas with excitement and joy for their accomplishments.

However, I also know some fine Christian people who have many heartaches with members of their families. They wanted to rock their grandchildren on their laps, but a rift developed during the early years of those youngsters' lives, and with a broken heart grandma/grandpa never got to hold those young children.

Sometimes a child gets married and it seems like the family events you hoped to have suddenly go to the other side of the family. Perhaps you experienced a nosey parent. Possibly you just drifted apart and the phone line just didn't seem to go in both directions! For whatever reason, you felt that a piece of your family was missing that you would never find again!

It hurts when your family does not share your point of view. It is even more devastating when they begin to doubt you and work against you. Family is supposed to be a safe place. But sometimes it doesn't work that way.

Jesus truly understands what this is like. We would think that Jesus as the perfect Son of God would never have family problems. We learn in Matthew 12, however, with help from Mark 3, that Jesus had a difficult time with his family. For all of the understanding Mary had about Jesus, and what she surely had to pass on to the family, John 7:5 teaches us, "For not even his brothers believed in him. (ESV)" How devastating it must have been and how joyous it could have been had Jesus had the support of his family!

Mark 3:21 tells us "And when his family heard it, they went out to seize him, for they were saying, 'He is out of his mind.'" This broad statement comes after Jesus has performed many miracles and called His disciples to Himself. Hold on to this thought for just a minute.

Back in one of my ministries, I spoke with a young man who was trying to decide what he wanted to do in life. And one of the things that he was considering was being a pastoral minister. He and I were discussing this when his father, a successful businessman in town and a leader of the church, told his son, point blank, "You don't want to do that. You want to be successful and make money." And a few years later, after I left that ministry, I found out the son had indeed gone into the family business. Family stood in the way of kingdom work.

Maybe you, like Jesus, have been challenged because of a ministry choice. Maybe your family doesn't understand why you belong to Jesus and serve Him in faithful worship and Sunday School attendance. Perhaps the gulf has been so great you can't see eye to eye about anything. You are alone in the quagmire of life. If this is where you are, could I invite you to take a look at how Jesus faced the rejection of his family? And even before we do, let me assure you that this all paid off.

Pick up that thought again about Jesus' family. Jesus' brothers did become followers probably even writing books of the Bible. And in that devastating moment on the cross, Jesus' mother remained firm until Jesus passed her care on to His best friend.

Jesus offers us some real help when it comes to the absence of the support of our family. I hope that a few of these ideas may help you when your heart is breaking.

First, don't get sidetracked in life, especially serving the Kingdom, even when you are dying inside because you feel all alone. In Matthew 12:46 we see that Jesus' family has come to fulfill their mission seen in Mark 3. They think Jesus is crazy and they want to take Him home.

Jesus knew the truth. He wasn't crazy. Satan wanted His family to think He was crazy to pull Him out of circulation. The way Jesus fought against this was to keep remembering what He was doing and why.

I don't know your situation. Maybe you have a spouse that does not understand your dedication. Or perhaps you are being persuaded that some event is coming up that is more important than the service you perform or the worship you attend. Could it possibly be that you are away from home and the person you are with does not "do" church and so you are kept away?

As I said in the preceding chapters don't lose your focus. And if you are, then try to refocus. You will find that when you do, maintaining your faith will be easier and you will sense more success in what you do.

Secondly, Jesus found strength by identifying other special people in His life. Note Matthew 12:48-50, "But he replied to the man who told him, 'Who is my mother, and who are my brothers?' (49) And stretching out his hand toward his disciples, he said, 'Here are my mother and my brothers! (50) For whoever does the will of my Father in heaven is my brother and sister and mother.'"

One of the biggest challenges of being in a located ministry is that frequently it is not close to home. That means the family resources often available when you are close to mom and dad and brothers and sisters simply aren't in place. And what do you do then?

During one of my earlier ministries, this was the case. We were at least two hours away from family. This was also the ministry where our two girls were born. With the handy telephone on the wall we could call and talk to our families and share the news of the day, but having their help just was not a possibility.

It seemed, however, that God had put just the right people across the street from us. Cliff was retired but that did not stop him from cleaning the church building and taking care of the heating system there. His wife Fran was a homemaker extraordinaire. She could cook a meal and make the most of all the fresh produce Cliff raised in his small, but productive, garden. She also made wonderful desserts. Allow me to change the punctuation on her desserts!!!!!!!!!

When we wanted a home cooked meal, Fran's kitchen and back porch dining table. were frequently open to us. Sure, we would have liked to have the homemade desserts and meals we were used to. My father-in-law, an avid fisherman, frequently did fish fries with some of the best homemade hush puppies you could imagine. And my mother-in-law made slaw so good it would make your tongue slap your brains out. But we found the delicacies at Cliff and Fran' house were prepared and presented with just as much flavor, and love, as we knew at home.

When I came down with the flu, it was Cliff who drove me to the hospital emergency room. When we needed an emergency baby sitter it was Fran who helped out. And it wasn't always in an emergency as they would watch the kids just as if they were flesh and blood. They never minded when our little ones decided they were going to bounce down the steps on their backsides, just for fun. And it was Cliff who always had a pocket full of pennies to reward our older daughter as she learned to count them.

I could probably regale you with Cliff and Fran stories for hours. This little trip down memory lane brings more of them to mind. But I won't do that to you. Instead, I may just give you a moment to think about someone in your life who is or was like family. Take just a moment to remember how they helped you. And take a moment to thank God for them and the difference they made in your life.

Thirdly, maybe your position in life is not to need the family, but to be family. In verse 50 in the scripture we just looked at, Jesus says that whoever does the will of the Father is like a brother or sister or mother.

Maybe you are past the place in life where you don't need grandmas and grandpas. Maybe you are at the place you can be like a grandma or grandpa.

In the decades that I have been alive, I have seen a fundamental shift in family. Where the classic family used to be mom and dad and kids with support family close by, we are seeing in our world, more single parent families. And even in the old definition of family, we are seeing tired moms and dads who are single and trying to do double duty to make sure the kids are cared for but just don't have the energy to do so. They could use a little help sometimes that you might be able to give.

Look beyond just "family with kids" and consider other situations where you might be able to help. Is there a widow or widower who could use a kind word and a visit? Does someone in town not have meals all the time? Are there neighbor children who don't know about Jesus that you could share Jesus with? Or could you possibly hold a backyard VBS at your place, so they can know Jesus, also?

I am convinced that we have not exhausted ministry opportunities. As days go by, new opportunities will undoubtedly open up we could not at possibly imagine right now. We must be ready to walk through those doors when they open.

Perhaps you have been praying that some family situation would clear itself up! Maybe you have tried to resolve the situation until you are blue in the face! You know it would take a miracle to bring everybody back together again! Don't give up praying about it! A decade down the road, the situation may resolve itself. I have seen it happen!

But remember that there are people like family out there who want to help or need your help. Don't refuse the blessing to accept their help, or give them help, a blessing for you and for them!

An Everyday Jesus for the Everyday Life – Chapter 3
A Close and Lasting Relationship
"When Friends Fail Us"

According to Paul Faulkner at "heartlight.org", "... all of us have a story, and all of us have a profound longing for friendship — a poignant searching for the kinds of things that only a close and lasting relationship can bring."[4]

The Proverb writer in chapter 18 and verse 24 reminds us, "One who has unreliable friends soon comes to ruin, but there is a friend who sticks closer than a brother." The Proverb writer understands that need for friendships too!

I guess Faulkner knew there were a lot of Franks out there, Franks who needed friends. You really had to see Frank to understand. He stood about 6' 3" tall, give or take an inch. He was the poster child for acne medicines as he had been terribly scarred with the disease as he grew. Frank wore glasses that were so thick, you could see the refraction in action from several feet away. To say he was uncoordinated was being polite. If Isaiah 53:2b wasn't about Jesus, it perfectly described Frank: "He had no beauty or majesty to attract us to him, nothing in his appearance that we should desire him."

Frank was in his first day in this new school. Most of the students giggled or laughed when he came by. Some remained politely quiet. Frank was here. He walked among us. The cold shoulder he received was dropping from chilly to freezing.

The guidance counselor, Mrs. Ratcliff, came to me one day shortly after Frank's appearance. Her speech started out something like this, "Randy, I know you are a Christian. I know you want to serve God. And I need your help." I knew something was up, but I didn't know what.

It did not take long to find out. Once the pleasantries were past, the rest came rolling out. "You've met Frank, haven't you, the new student? Well, I was hoping you would agree to spend some time with him. You don't have to be best friends or anything, but Frank needs someone to talk to. Would you do it?"

What could I say? Back in the "pre-T-rex" days, you just didn't tell a respected teacher that you wouldn't do something, unless you wanted trouble. So, I told her that I would. Mrs. Ratcliff seemed pleased. She was wearing one of those smiles like a used car salesman gives you to close the deal. I figured that I could say hello a couple of times, be interested in him, and everybody would be happy. And, after all, isn't that what a Christian was supposed to do?

Next day, I passed Frank in the hall. I smiled and said hello. He looked at me, surprised! I found it didn't hurt to talk to Frank. I started looking for chances to connect with Frank after that. He did the best he could to dodge the heavy student traffic between classes as we walked and talked. Me, I just mowed the other students down trying to keep up with him.

All this was working out okay. . .until! Until some of the guys in my class cornered me, sans Frank. "Hey, Randy! We see you are hanging around with Frank." Without hardly room for me to breathe "Yes", their carefully plotted script continued. They proceeded to tell me that Frank had come to our school fresh out of reform school. They asked me if I was aware I was hanging around with a jail bird! As I turned my back to leave they snickered!

I fell for it. I was incensed. I was embarrassed by my classmates. I had been used by the guidance counselor! I didn't feel so kindly toward Frank because of his newly revealed sin! But, secretly I hurt inside because I needed a friend too, because sometimes I felt as lonely as Frank looked.

Mrs. Ratcliff knew the minute I stormed into the guidance office that something wasn't right. She asked me in her straightforward, no nonsense way what the problem was. And I let go with both barrels. In short order the real issue came out: "Why didn't you tell me he had been in reform school? I should have known before I started all this."

The used car salesman smile was gone! In fact, with a stern look on her face, she laid it out on the line. I remember most of the words she said because she said a lot in a few words, "Do you know what Frank was in reform school for? He stole one candy bar at the grocery store!" She reminded me that Frank had always had a different life. He was always teased. Usually he was ignored. And then she played the Christian card – Christians love people and strive to help them. I always hated when people did that.

But I hated myself at that point in time, too. I had let God down. I had let Frank down. I had let me down. I played into the mean plan of the guys and their speech! I did not like what I saw. How could I face Frank the next day? How could I ever explain my motivation and my foolishness?

Turns out I didn't have to. Frank wasn't at school the next day, or the next day, or the next. Frank was gone. I mentally gave myself the licking of my life.

Before you tell me not to be too hard on myself, let me assure you that this incident has become the one I learned the most from, so all was not lost. And besides, there have been times when I, too, have been let down by friends. I hope that I responded as graciously as Jesus did when He was let down by His friends, as graciously as I hoped Frank would toward me.

When you look at the circle of influence that Jesus had, you might be quite amazed to realize that His circle looks a lot like a circle you or I might have. When you walk down the street of your hometown, you will pass people that you don't know, people that you know but don't spend much time with, people that you know well and enjoy talking to, and those people that you feel very comfortable with, ones you can tell anything to, ones you can be honest with.

When Jesus walked on the earth, there were many times in the crowd of people when those around pushed and shoved just to see the famous teacher. However, they were not friends. There were people that Jesus knew that He might speak to everyday. There were people like Mary and Martha and Lazarus whom he knew well and spent time with. Then there were the twelve and within that group Peter and James and John, the ones He seemed to spend those personal moments with, the ones who saw all the special things, the ones who received all the insights and the intimate moments that friends share together.

That friendship was soon challenged when Jesus was finally in the hands of the government. Luke 22:54-62 tells us when one of His friends, let Him down. It was Peter, of course. Three times in this passage, Peter denies Jesus. That's what friends do, right? When someone you know and love is in trouble, and you want to save your hide, you disassociate yourself from them.

The first denial was that of Peter to a young woman sitting around the charcoal fire on a cool night, as Jesus is being dragged in for judgement. Peter's words were, "Woman, I don't even know that man!" (CEV – Luke 22:57). In verses 58 and 60 of that same chapter, Jesus relates to two men that he did not know this Jesus. The phrases go like this: "No, I'm not!" and "I don't know what you are talking about."

If I were Jesus, I would probably have been very unkind to Peter. I would scream about how we had been friends. I would remind him of all the things we had done together. I would have made a scene until I felt vindicated in my complaining.

Fortunately, Jesus did not treat His friends that way, even after they let Him down. Just before the rooster crowed, as He said it would, Jesus simply looked at Peter. I am guessing it was the look that says, "How could you do that?" The look melted Peter into puddles of shame, disgrace, and embarrassment. I believe that Peter probably was giving himself a licking that day, just like I did over Frank.

But the beauty of the friendship of Christ was that Jesus did not hold a grudge and still wanted His friend to experience wholeness so he could be a great worker for the kingdom. John 21 tells the story of Jesus appearing to His disciples after the resurrection. The disciples did not know who Jesus was at the time, but Jesus addresses them. In the NIV translation and in the NIrV translation, Jesus calls them friends. But most of the other translations notice the fact that

Jesus uses a term of endearment addressing children or maybe even those young in faith.

Peter soon realizes after they pull in a net full of fish that it is Jesus who is on the bank. And now Peter, who denied his friend, is the first to get to Him. After fellowshipping around a meal of fish, Jesus pulls Peter aside and helps Peter to see the friendship is not broken, no matter the sin.

Three times in helping Peter pick up the friendship pieces Jesus asks about love. In our English translations, it is hard to tell the difference. The Greek words offer a little better understanding of the passage. The first two times Jesus asks Peter about his love, the word Jesus uses in the word agape — the kind of love that wants what is best for the other, no matter the cost. Each of those times, Peter answered that he loved the Lord as a friend, a different Greek word which we say is philos (brotherly love, city of Philadelphia for example).

The third time, Jesus feeds back what Peter is saying when he asks Peter if Peter loves Him as a friend. No wonder Peter is upset! But his answer is still the same when he says that he does love the Lord as a friend. And that seemed to be what Jesus was looking for to help get Peter back from his disappointment about himself.

This is how Jesus restored a friend who denied Him. It is a beautiful story. It has a happy ending compared to the tragic tale about one of Jesus' other disciples.

Judas Iscariot is a name that will live in infamy. He is known as the disciple of Jesus who sold Jesus into the hand of the enemy for 30 pieces of silver. The sign of betrayal was already made; Judas would kiss the man the guards were looking for.

Judas walks right up to Jesus and Jesus says these words, "My friend, why are you here?" With that, Jesus gets a kiss from Judas, and the guard take Jesus to meet his destiny. For the betrayal that Judas makes, Jesus says remarkably little.

The one thing that is necessary to note here is in the usage of the word "friend" basically used in each translation I could find. The Greek word here is different than the previous. This Greek word translated friend is a word that means "comrade" or "people who have struggled together". It shows a unique and special relationship. If, for example, you ask men who served in the military in the past about their "comrades" there is always a special bond. It was a bond that was forged through striving and sweating and suffering together. And that was the word Jesus used here in relationship to Judas.

Again, there is no name calling. There is no questioning sanity. Perhaps it is because Jesus has accepted His fate and knows what is coming. But even in betrayal the forgiveness of Jesus radiates toward this misguided soldier-friend named Judas. The misguided soldier-friend is not so forgiving of himself and meets his end, at his own hand, in a noose. Perhaps it is easier for friends to forgive than for the betrayers to forgive themselves.

There were more times than just these two. When the disciples could not stay awake to pray with Jesus in the garden, He asked them about it, but understood their human nature and let it go. And even in the time of His crucifixion, Jesus words of prayer to His Father were for forgiveness because the people and the guards had no idea what was going on. Even though they were not His friends He treated them like friends. What a marvelous Savior and example!

The names Shipley, Scroggins, and Scott probably don't mean much to you. But to the people of the small community in which I live, these three names stand for bravery, honor, and valor. A granite memorial has been erected by the high school gym door, so that people will never forget what those 3 did. Their faces shine forth as a reminder to our people that these three men were friends of the community. Between the years of 1968 and 1973, Scroggins, Scott, and Shipley, died in the conflict in Viet Nam. And they are honored even today as men remembered and loved by their community.

Etched on the granite you will find a memorial reading that I want to share part of. "Not for fame or reward, Not for place or for rank, Not lured by ambition, Or goaded by necessity, But in simple obedience to duty, As they understood it, These men suffered all, Sacrificed all, Dared all, and Died."

Isn't that the message that Jesus taught and exemplified as seen in John 15:13 "Greater love has no one than this: to lay down one's life for one's friends"? Of course, in the next verse Jesus specifies that His friends are those who do what He commands. But somewhere along the way, that definition of friendship expands. Jesus sees that His sacrifice is necessary. And so He looks past the denial of Peter, the sleepiness of the disciples, and even the torture of the guards to be a friend. There is no condemnation, only the hope that they will understand the plan of God that He brings, and accept it so that He might share with His friends for all eternity.

Next time someone abuses your friendship, or even denies it, or when you aren't such a good friend yourself, could I encourage you to let the friendship of Jesus color your response? It is amazing how that view of things can and will change the world! It can help you develop that "close and lasting relationship for which we all long"!

An Everyday Jesus for the Everyday Life – Chapter 4
Giving Back to Caesar
"When Government Confounds Us"

The outside of the envelope said that the letter had come from the City of Chicago. I asked myself what was so important that the city of Chicago would be writing me a letter. Opening it up, I soon found out. I was the proud owner of a parking ticket for parking with an expired meter.

It was a rather comical matter because I had not been in Chicago for 20 years. And, I had never, ever driven a car in Chicago. I had flown in one trip and taken a bus the other. I wondered if someone could have taken my car without me realizing it. But no, the plate number they claimed was there, had not been there. And the description of the vehicle with the plate on it did not even come close to matching mine. After some back-and-forth correspondence, I guess I must have convinced them. Especially when I found out that the meter officer had really transposed two of the numbers. Then it all made sense. And we finally dealt with all the issues.

I am very thankful for the systems of government that we enjoy in our country. And I am proud to be a part of the land of the free and the home of the brave. But that system sometimes simply confounds us. We aren't sure how to especially deal with it. I was even more confounded by the City of Chicago in that about 4 years later, I received another parking ticket. Human error, obviously. Frustration through a government entity, no doubt!

Sometimes the confounding from the government is at a lot higher stakes. Enter Mary Surrat. Mrs. Surrat ran a boarding house in Washington, D.C. during the time President Lincoln was in office. John Wilkes Booth, who later actually did assassinate President Lincoln, was a frequent guest at her boarding house. Mrs. Surrat's family members did conspire with Booth and a plan was hatched not only to kill Lincoln, but to go after Vice-President Andrew Johnson and other members of the cabinet. However, history has never proven that Mrs. Surrat was a part of the plan other than allowing weapons storage and clandestine meetings to take place at the boarding house.

When all was said and done, Mrs. Surrat was arrested and kept confined in the old Arsenal Penitentiary. She was found guilty in the military tribunal and given a reserved spot on the gallows where the conspirators would die. In fact, history says that she was the first woman executed by hanging by the federal government.

Many historians now believe that Mary Surrat was let down by her government. Many people tried to intercede on her behalf. Her son, John Surratt, escaped to Canada and did not try to intercede on her behalf; he apparently was guilty. And Preston King, who had become part of President Johnson's staff, kept all requests for her clemency away from the President. King later tied a bag of bullets around his neck and jumped off a ferry boat never to be seen again.[5] Mary Surrat was physically, and literally, let down by her government in the minds of many.

I began writing this chapter sitting under our church pavilion. It was a beautiful day with a clear blue sky, a few wispy clouds blowing by. Sitting on my laptop, was a strange little bug. I know it was a bug but it reminded me of a teeny-tiny frog.

Now before you think I have lost my senses, it is the strange action of the bug that caught my attention. It turned around to face me, at least I guess I was looking at its face. And then it began a peculiar kind of dance. With its four legs firmly planted on the computer, this masterpiece of God began to lean to its left, and then to its right, then to its left, then to its right bouncing as it went. The dance went on for several seconds in the same routine. Then, as if bored, it began doing something different and then it was gone from my sight.

I have concluded that God showed me the swaying of the bug to help me visualize what modern government has become and why government is so confounding. In this land of the free and home of the brave, in our land of democracy, government has been in a constant sway.

Depending on who power brokers our federal government or our state or commonwealth legislatures, the legislative path moves to the "left" or more liberal. With a change in power brokers, the legislative path moves to the "right" or more conservative. The dance continues as the powerbrokers continue their changing and we often feel caught in the confusion.

In the United States of America, we the people seem confounded by the government approach to insurance, taxes, moral issues, and more. Some of the issues that we face are truly political issues. How taxes are assessed may concern us, but that process does not have eternal significance. However, issues such as the life of an unborn child, the needs of small children, taking care of the elderly, and sexual preference also are addressed by government bodies and confound many Christians who are trying to understand how to live in a country, a world, or any smaller unit of government, where the norm has drifted so far from where it used to be. And so far from what it seems God's plan might be.

How do Christians deal with these confounding issues? How would Jesus say to deal with a government where lives of Christians are injured or destroyed because of faith? I wonder what He would say when homes are taken and property is ripped away from people who love Him?

If you stop and think about it, Jesus was let down by the government of His day. Pilate became a wimp while an overbearing Caiaphas and Annas manipulated the system to finally bring an end, so they thought, to their enemy Jesus. This was political corruption at its finest. Though it had the end of meeting God's plan, there was nothing fair about it.

Similarly, others in the faith of Christ were treated unfairly also. Later Christians were thrown to the lions and left in pits. They were tortured because of their faith. Hebrews gives us an account of how government affected Christians in an unfair way. Note Hebrews 11:36-37: "Some faced jeers and flogging, and even chains and imprisonment. (37) They were put to death by stoning; they were sawed in two, they were killed by the sword. They went about in sheepskins and goatskins, destitute, persecuted and mistreated. . ." The mistreatment of Christians has always been there and always applied unfairly. Talk about confounding!

It would be very nice if there were some kind of miracle that could just happen and make everything better. It would be so great if all the moral issues and tax issues and political issues and everything related to government could be fixed in one snap of the fingers. How wonderful if one prayer would fix everything that needs to be fixed.

But instead, Jesus gave us some teachings that we need to understand if we want to figure out how to deal with the government confounding us. I am confident when we understand and apply these principles, we will have no trouble being able to endure everything the government might do to us.

First, we must realize the ultimate source of government. Where does government come from? How can that help us when government is confounding us?

Jesus' comment to Pilate at His hearing is an important one. John 19:11 says, "You would have no authority over me unless it had been given you from above." Paul reflects on that in Romans 13:1b, "There is no authority except from God, and those that exist have been instituted by God."

I truly wish I understood why the Hitlers were allowed to rule! I also wish I could understand why some of the political enemies of Christians in the middle east are still there injuring and killing our brothers in Christ. Why do these political maniacs have it in their hearts to do wickedness? Why do our brothers and sisters in Christ get persecuted?

I don't have the answer. But I can be sure that those rulers are put there by God. God used extremely wicked kings in the Old Testament to carry out His way. Fortunately, some of those kings came to understand God in a better way than many of His own people. And the whole situation made His people realize the wrongs and start standing for the right.

I admit this is my own glorified thinking, but at times it seems that Christian people check their brains at the door.

Everything is under control. I don't have to have any convictions or take a stand for my beliefs. It will all come out okay.

When Joshua and Caleb were under the gun from the other spies and the people of God about the ability to enter the promised land, they stood for what was right, even though people were against them. This political exploit opened their eyes to the power of God even when they seemed outnumbered.

John the Baptist stood against Herod for having his brother's wife. It cost him his life, but John saw that people must take a stand to state what is God's way, even to those leaders God put into power.

Secondly it is good to hear Jesus' words in Mark 12:17, "Then Jesus said to them, 'Give back to Caesar what is Caesar's and to God what is God's.' And they were amazed at him." Of course, when you read the text here you see this is about the taxes being paid. But I had never noticed before the phrase "give back". Upon researching it a little bit, this is the best translation of the Greek word. It implies the source of the money is Caesar. Caesar gave you the coinage, so give back what is his. But it also implies the same thing about God. Out of what God gave you, you are only giving back.

In the traps the Pharisees and others set for Jesus, their hope had been that Jesus would make the Roman government mad thereby giving opportunity to say that Jesus was a traitor. And they knew that traitors would be dealt with sharply.

But that was never part of Jesus' plan. Jesus understood that there was a place for government, that in fact it was necessary. And in looking back at Jesus, he always used the utmost care, even providing the coinage for the temple tax from the mouth of a fish. Jesus knew that with its road systems and ability to communicate most anywhere in the world, Rome could be a grand ally if used as designed.

But He also knew that to pick up the banner of traitor or rabble-rouser would be a role Rome would never understand. And so, He carefully did what needed to be done in respect. In fact, the only time that I have seen that Jesus was ever disrespectful was when the Jewish leaders refused to serve as they should have, when they were more interested in themselves and their positions.

And even when Jesus was talking about His kingdom, you will find that He never disrespects this very crooked Roman government and its way of getting things done. Unfair things happen.

As Christians, how can we use these principles to help us when the government confounds us? Are there really answers for us today? I believe so.

One of the principles we uncovered is that the governments that we have today are put into place by God Himself. That offers us some guiding principles.

The first principle is that because these are God's messengers, these people should be treated with the utmost respect. They should be treated like we would expect ourselves to treat God. Many times, people yell unflattering remarks at leaders. Some even call them unkind names. And sadly, many Christians are involved in the name calling. We may not care for some of the leaders, but we will find that we are far better off when we treat them with respect, even when we strongly disagree with their policies. This is a very unique opportunity in the democracy in which we live. It is also the example that Jesus lived out.

In the beginning of this chapter, I spoke about getting the parking tickets. My initial thought was to give those people in Chicago a piece of my mind. I have not been there in 20 years. I never had a car in your city. You people are just so dumb. But by offering disrespect, I can have a difficult time getting a hearing and might never get a real problem fixed because of my attitude. And if I have to answer to God for my behavior, . . . well, that is a situation I just don't want or need in my life.

The Golden Rule applies as well. I should treat people as I want to be treated. That is simply part of what the Christian life is all about. It really works. And it doubly applies here.

The other principle was to give back to Caesar what is Caesar's and give back to God the things that are God's. I feel this principle really needs some attention in our lives.

One of the great things about this country is the ability we have to speak up about things that concern us. The good thing is that we as Christians can make our case. The sad dilemma is that everybody gets to be heard and sometimes we must live with issues that we are uncomfortable with. I am convinced we need to use this principle to make sure people understand God's way. It may not always be appreciated, but it needs to be out there. We have the right to let these leaders know what our concerns are. Many doubt it makes much difference but if we have a right and don't use it, we might soon see ourselves lose it.

Another thing we can do, and should do, is to pay the taxes we are responsible for. I do agree that we get taxed too much and in wrong manners. But our government must have the resources to operate. Do I feel there is abuse? Certainly! But if we do our part to expose problems and our leaders reject our proposals, we have the right to reject them at the next ballot box. And if they are truly crooked, they will have to answer for their misdeeds before the Father who allowed them to be in such a position.

Okay, Randy, I get what you say. But what about people who live in lands where there is no democracy? What about the places where Christians have family taken away or where they have property destroyed or if they are executed because of their faith? What then?

That is truly a tough call! Jesus showed restraint in dealing with the government, even in positions where His life was on the line. We can pray that such governments will change their minds. We know that Satan has influence in a lot of leaders, so as Christians we must expect tough times. We know those times are coming. In the meantime, we can encourage our brothers and sisters in Christ to stand firm and offer any help we can when the persecution is heavy. It behooves us to follow the example of our Savior in every situation.

Back in the early 1970's, when I was 19 years old, the Viet Nam war was starting to slow down. A draft system was still in place. For those who might not know about the draft, young men, usually around age 19 were conscripted by drawing numbers related to their birthdays and sent into the military. In 1972, the last year for the draft, my birthday, October 14 was chosen to have a lottery draw of #14. What that meant was I had to report to my draft board because my date was so close to the top of the list. The draft board in my county would then choose when I would go to be evaluated for service. And it would be soon!

I don't deny that I did not want to go to Viet Nam. Most young men did not want to go. But if I were chosen, I would have to render to Caesar what was his and that would include a trip to Viet Nam to fight. And not long after the lottery for the draft, I received a letter that I would have to report to Indianapolis draft center for a physical. I failed my physical! But had I passed I would have been required to enter the military and go fight for my country.

I didn't yell or scream about the unfairness of it all. Nor did I do what a lot of young men did and head for Canada to avoid the draft. I left myself in the system to do what needed to be done and God made the choice for me. I did not go, but I would have.

I don't understand why so many things opposed to God are active in the world today. I don't know why wrong is called right and right is called wrong. But this I vow, and hope you will too, that I will use my rights in a respectful way to lift up Christ and His way! And when the government seems to be confounding, I will look to the example of Jesus to help me figure what route to go to meet the challenge.

An Everyday Jesus for the Everyday Life – Chapter 5
Finding Joy at Work
"When Work Demoralizes Us"

I really never liked having board meetings on Sunday mornings. Most of the time the meetings go all right. But every once in a while, meetings turn sour. Moving into Sunday School or Worship and praising God are the farthest things from your mind after meetings like those. One meeting I attended topped them all!

Most of the board members were present that day. The meeting was grim by any standard. The minutes were read and reports given. The next matter of business became the surprise dismissal of the minister, me. The business was pretty well cut and dried. The board chairman had memorized his script. He intoned that he knew we had a 60-day contract and the church would fulfill the terms of the contract. But...and it was a BIG but, this day would end my preaching at the church. After the morning message, I would announce I was leaving and I would never return to the pulpit of this church. I had a couple of days to get the office cleaned out when no one else was present. I would move out of the parsonage within the 60 days of my contract. The message was that most of the leadership washed their hands of me!

My head was spinning! What was I going to do? I had only 60 days to do something. I did not understand why all this happened. Certainly no one charged me with any moral wrongdoing. The most that I could figure was that I had upset someone's apple cart.

But the cause did not matter. No amount of discussion, pleading, or begging would change anything. I had the responsibility to explain to my wife and to my two small daughters, in just the hour between the meeting and the service, that we were going to have to leave after only a few short months in this ministry.

This whole situation led me to doubt myself. I hinted, no yelled, to myself that I just wasn't a very good preacher. I felt I had failed in being the pastor/shepherd to the church. My gut began to tell me that it was time to quit the ministry and begin looking for other work. I would never be a pastor again! Most importantly, did God even love me? Did He see me as a failure too?

Perhaps you have been demoralized by a job situation you are in or have been in. Your self-worth has been shattered. You have been fired or demoted or perhaps even ignored. You have been led to believe that you have no value to the company. You believe that all the years of service you have put in, sometimes sacrificially, have gone down the drain. You have questioned yourself and your future. What will you tell your wife and children? How can you ever look at your own face in the mirror again because you just know that all you see is someone who failed?

Your problem might not be a firing or being released from a job. Perhaps you find people take advantage of your good work and your good nature. Maybe you feel under appreciated. Possibility you can't identify the issue but getting up out of bed to go to work has become more of a struggle than ever. You just don't want to go because the climate in which you work has become mundane and lacks fulfillment. In one recent survey, less than 50% of the respondents reported being satisfied with their jobs. It had been the same way in that survey for the previous 8 years.[6]

Having such feelings toward work can be very disconcerting, especially since we are seemingly hard wired to need to do work. Being in God's image allows us to understand this.

God our creator was Himself a worker. We see that he created the world in 6 days, taking the 7th day to rest. In the Bible, God shares with us how we should feel about work. In Ecclesiastes 2:24 we read, "A person can do nothing better than to eat and drink and find satisfaction in their own toil. This too, I see, is from the hand of God." And Ecclesiastes 3:12-13 reminds us, "I know the best thing we can do is to always enjoy life, (13) because God's gift to us is the happiness we get from our food and drink and from the work we do." We learn from 2Thessalonians 3:10 that work is really a part of the discipline of our lives, "We also gave you the rule that if you don't work, you don't eat."

What do we do to satisfy this hard wiring job when it seems we are failing at it? How do we regroup to find purpose for our lives? Since I don't know of any miraculous plan that will get you back to work, or make a boss give you back a job, let's look at some of the simple teachings of Jesus that can sustain you when the world fails us concerning work. Here are some hints that may help you.

Hint number one would be this, when you are facing a tough time in your work situation, why not put Matthew 6:33-34 on a note card on your bathroom mirror. I recommend putting it on the mirror so when you look in that mirror, wanting to beat yourself up for being such a failure, you can be reminded of how to get through troubling times. Matthew

6:33-34 reminds us, "But put God's kingdom first. Do what he wants you to do. Then all of those things will also be given to you. (34) So don't worry about tomorrow. Tomorrow will worry about itself. Each day has enough trouble of its own. (NIrV)"

I have discovered that the time when I feel the most disappointed with myself is when I have begun doing work for work's sake and have quit looking at work as part of the broad plan of serving God. That's not to say that I lost my job because I quit serving God. When I was working for the church in the opening story, I really was trying to be tuned into what it seemed God wanted me to do in this ministry.

But I did learn from practical experience and the above scripture. When work is an issue, it is necessary to look at your motive for working and see if God is being put first in your work situation. That does not mean to work for free. It does mean asking yourself if your overriding goal in working is to find a way to present yourself as a servant of Christ. It does mean you will be honest and forthright in your dealings with your employer. It does mean you will be on time for your work and present a good example for others in your job without shoving it in their faces. It does mean you will not look like a lot of other people in the work force. It seems modern thought goes against good work ethic that is so necessary in the working world today. It does mean that even if your employer is not shooting straight with you that you will ALWAYS shoot square with him/her.

I am sure if you have been given a pink slip, this might be one of the harder things to do. But it is vital to be sure that God, not your job, is in the center of your life! It can make a world of difference as you work, or when you work again.

Hint 2 is a little different. When you get tired of looking at the card on the bathroom mirror, take it down and put this verse up there: Matthew 11:28 reminds us, "Come to me, all of you who are tired and are carrying heavy loads. I will give you rest."

I took some time to do a little research on two of the Greek words in this text. One of those is the word used for "tired". The Greek implies a person who is fatigued from hard work. If you are the kind of person who puts all the effort you can in working, you have worked yourself until you are tired and want to drop, wondering if it is worth it all, this promise is for you. I realize it does not only mean working at a job, but it does apply in this situation.

The second word was about the phrase relating to "carrying heavy loads". The word picture here is of the beast of burden who is overloaded. It is the image of an animal struggling to do what it has to do because it is trying to carry too much. Maybe you are burdened because you don't have a job. Or maybe you are overburdened because you feel you are doing your work and the work of others. That makes you feel alone, like an ox in a yoke without a partner. Again, this scripture is not just about earthly jobs, but it certainly applies to His children who are doing their best as they long for a moment's peace.

The promise is "rest". It does not promise a vacation to beautiful far away islands, nor does it say you will never have any more worries. But it seems to me He is saying that we can have a brief get away from those problems of the world. We can have a chance to breathe and pull everything back together. He can give us those moments we so desperately need. This scripture promises the greatest rest of all, some place to rest with Him, forever, where earthly labor needs done no more.

Maybe you are saying, "But I have a pink-slip. I don't have a job to change my attitude about." Then I would encourage you to become familiar with the unfaithful steward. Some translations call him the unfaithful manager. The scripture is Luke 16:1-13.

Before you even read it, let me warn you that this is not a step by step plan to follow. The reason I say that is because we see the manager doing something that was not illegal, but not good in the eyes of the master. The steward was still in charge. Whatever he said in the affairs of the master was still binding because he had not been taken off the job. But what is demonstrated is not good stewardship and would make the owner pretty upset.

The manager told each of the debtors to the master to change their bills as to what they owed. He was making friends by giving favors to these men. Then, they would like him and he would be welcomed by them. Even the master said that he was a pretty sharp cookie, actually very clever, in what he did. The Master did not like it, but he saw the steward had a brain and could use it.

The point is that the Unfaithful manager had a plan to deal with his pink slip. He did not wallow in self-pity...too much! Though it may be very hard to do, when facing a pink slip, do your best to come up with a plan that will help you through the rough times. It may not be a perfect plan. It may not be the plan you want. Having a plan gives you something to focus on when you feel dejected. It gives you a reason to keep digging for new work. It gets you past the despair that overwhelms and takes away self-worth.

At the time I was let go from the church, I sought something to do while seeking another church. One job actually came to me. A local aluminum smelter needed an overnight watch man for a couple of weekends. And later, as Christmas came closer, I got a job overnight stocking shelves at a chain toy store in a nearby city. The added benefit was I could buy my small daughters' toys at a discount for the upcoming Christmas. Part of my plan was to find something, anything that I could do, that would help keep my family going. Instead of despair, I kept trusting in hope!

What I know is that the job market is hard! I know that people work at jobs they were never prepared for. People work at jobs they don't like. But they do it because they have a plan and work the plan. I wish I could say why some families have to go through long stretches time of trying to find a job that will work. And I don't know why these do. I know countless younger and older families who could not seemingly find the most basic of jobs. But let me encourage you, if you are facing such a situation, to be clever. If you can help someone with what you have, you will network and make a friend, and maybe even make a difference for all eternity whenever you trust God to make the difference in your life.

Above all, don't give up. Keep looking up! Keep on your plan! Not having work, or not having the kind of work you really like, is probably only temporary. But don't be surprised when God does something you never imagined in your life.

I attended Bible college for four years training to be a preacher/pastor. And in the passing decades in which I have lived God has moved me into a number of roles, not pertaining to being a preacher/pastor. I cleaned municipal buildings. I worked in a couple of radio stations. I sold shoes and also Christian books. The job that surprised me the most was in fast food. To the day of this writing, I seek to keep my hand in that business, doing what I can in an ever-changing world and I have a marvelous boss who has been both boss and friend. Who would have ever thought?

One of the joys of that ministry, which seemed so much like a failure, was that the church I served did not have Sunday evening services. Since Sunday evenings were open, we chose to visit another congregation in that town that did have Sunday night worship. It was different than anything my family was used to. As we got acquainted with the people in that congregation, we found a warmth and love that we had never felt in the church that I served. It did not hurt that one of their leaders of the church we visited, was a man we had known from a previous ministry who had moved into this area.

When this church heard about our need, one of the men immediately allowed us to stay, rent free, in an extra house he had. This church also offered us some needed financial resources and food if we needed it. We had great fellowship times going out for ice cream. And our children were just the ages of some of the children in the church; close friendships were forged.

Many of our friends in this new church hoped that we could stay and be a part of their fellowship. It seems that God had other ideas. After a couple of interviews and visits with other churches, we finally moved from that area and our new friends. But God had in mind a ministry where we have had more than 30 years of influence on the church, although we actually spent 24 years plus in direct service to it. I have a feeling that had we tried to push and butt our own way through, we might never have known the blessing that God provided. Had we wallowed in our despair, I sense the same outcome.

I am not the fatalistic type! But I do believe that God can work through people who have their hearts set on the kingdom, who trust Him so they don't stress to death, and who learn how to plan for difficult times in the working, or lack of working, world. When your mind is open, it is amazing what you can see God doing! He really can make all things work for the good of those who love him! (Romans 8:28a)

> *An Everyday Jesus for the Everyday Life – Chapter 6*
> ## Oodles of Noodles
> *"When Money Lets You Down"*

I looked at the little yellow station wagon that sat in my driveway. It was like part of the family, the first new vehicle my wife and I had purchased since our marriage. The purchase seemed very practical. A true family car, it was destined to see us make trips into many parts of our great country.

But now there was a tear in my eye. I had figured that in about 3 weeks or so, the bank, as a lien holder, would be stopping by to pick the car up. It had been more than two months since I had been able to make a car payment. And they suggested that three months would be the most they could wait.

I had hoped that all the promises that had been made about work would be fulfilled. When I started at the fast food restaurant you read about in the introduction, there was a promise that I would be moved up into management. Now, nearly 6 months later, that promise had not been kept. Hours were long and hard as a crew person. The pay was barely manageable. The hot nights had been miserable. I heard the same songs, night after night, on the music channel piped through the store's music system. I was getting dissatisfied and depressed, watching and waiting for things to happen.

The little church that I was pastoring had an attendance of less than 20. They had managed to pull together some funds that allowed us to live in an old mobile home which sat on the church property. We were thankful for that mobile home because we had been living with a lady in the community who had some spare room in her home. But as nice as she was, we were just rubbing one another the wrong way. It had been a long time since she had little children in her house.

As far as we could see, there was nothing more. We tried to save the money we made from the church and the restaurant to keep food on the table. I know even at that, the cans in the pantry were sparse. My wife and girls ate as best they could. I would bring food home from the restaurant whenever possible. We tried to get a few Happy Meals when we could and take the girls to play at the play land at the restaurant. The local park was free, and I have some treasured pictures of the girls when they were small, crawling on the backs of turtles and alligators, sliding down slides, riding dizzying merry-go-rounds, all the while those cute little lips smiling with great joy.

Another week or so in toward the deadline, there was a Thanksgiving meeting and dinner at the church building. What I have failed to tell you to this point is that the property the church owned was an old public-school building. I have lots of stories that I would love to share about that, but maybe some other time. Also using this building, were some wonderful people who wanted to have a Christian School. They had consulted with the church prior to my taking a ministry there and the Christian School was born. Our children later attended there and my wife worked there.

The teachers of the Christian school knew of our situation. Apparently, they had passed the word on to some of the Christian families in the school who decided after the

Thanksgiving meeting, they were going to help the Whitehead family. That, my friends, was the night of the noodles. Some of the folks brought left over food. I remember green beans, and mashed potatoes, and chicken and NOODLES. Oodles and oodles of noodles! We ate them like manna and quail!

On top of that, the folks at the school had a food shower for us. Canned vegetables now sat in our pantry. There was fruit. There was soup. There was canned pasta. The bare little pantry was now overflowing. So were the tears in my eyes.

In just a matter of a few days the restaurant promotion unexpectedly came through. And someplace, I don't remember where, extra funds came in to start making the back payments on our yellow station wagon. The Lord provided so abundantly that I can't even remember all the details now, except that, the yellow station wagon continued to sit in our driveway and to offer us more adventures which I will also save for another time.

I keep thinking each chapter gets harder to write! But I think this might be the winner because dealing with finances, even when you have oodles of noodles, is always tough. I see that though I have been through some trying and difficult times when it comes to finances, there are still some areas that I can mature in. So, I guess this is for me as well as for you. The opening story reminds me that God has worked. And now I need to look at the teachings of Jesus to see what I can learn when my money lets me down. When there is no visible miracle on the horizon what can I learn that will help me until some answer does come?

Matthew chapter 6 sets right in the middle of Jesus' Sermon on the Mount. In my mind, if there is any one place in the scripture that consolidates the hopes and dreams and guidance of Jesus for His church, this would be the one place to go. Let's look at a couple of scriptures that would help us understand what to do or know when money fails us.

In the scripture where Jesus teaches His disciples how to pray, Jesus begins by showing His followers how to communicate with God. It is here that Jesus demonstrates the Fatherhood and care of God. He teaches them to seek forgiveness of sin as they forgive others. And He shows them how to seek to be kept away from evil.

One line, however, addresses what we need to ask God for. We see in this verse, Matthew 6:11, "Give us today our daily bread." Amid all the worries of this world, Jesus reminds us that the best thing we can do is to ask God for the things we need, food being chief among them.

I confess that when my family was going through a difficult time, I was not always zeroed in to the truth of this verse. It was hard for me to pick out what I really had to have. I did NOT have to have a fancy vehicle, though I needed transportation for my jobs. I did NOT have to have a new or better home; I needed shelter to protect my family. I did NOT have to have a 7-course meal, but I needed food to sustain us when we got hungry. We could not live without that.

From a more modern mindset, what might be some other things we seem to need. A good cell phone program almost seems a must where a simple one-line, multi-party phone used to do the job. Where we used to put up an antenna on our roof, now it seems satellite dishes come as a need in order to have the TV most people enjoy.

Do I have to have a smart phone with many Gigabytes of data? No, not really! Do I have to have satellite or cable TV or some similar media? No, I don't. I know several people who do not have that sort of media, though they may connect on social media on the internet.

I am aware of one family where the mom and dad have chosen to have a camper so they can take their children camping. In making this choice, husband and wife agreed that the wife would work to pay for this so mom, dad, and kids can spend time together away from distractions. This is nice. Is it a necessity? No, and I don't think they chose to look at it that way. But they did feel it was important. Is it something to be prayed about and asked for? Yes! Prayer would be helpful to understand the wisdom of doing what they were doing and in choosing a vehicle to serve them. But no, I am sure most would not think it falls in the category of daily bread.

Daily bread is what is needed to survive. In our story, we needed food, we needed shelter, and we needed the provision of forgiveness of sin through Christ. That was what we could count on God to provide when times were tough! That is what Jesus said to pray for!

Biggest problem? When we find ourselves in these situations where we are lacking, we probably worry (there is that word again!) about it. I have! I can't sleep. I can't plan. I can't dream. And it is all because worry is really what I am doing and not asking.

Take a look at this part of Matthew 6:31-33: "So do not worry, saying, 'What shall we eat?' or 'What shall we drink?'

or 'What shall we wear?' (32) For the pagans run after all these things, and your heavenly Father knows that you need them. (33) But seek first his kingdom and his righteousness, and all these things will be given to you as well." (NIV)

I have discovered from experience, that when I am worrying it is extremely difficult to seek God's kingdom first. I guess we can't really blame ourselves too much because of our self-preservation instincts. But perhaps we can find a way to channel that worry into something more positive, especially us Kingdom people.

We might do well to take the advice of Jesus when we feel worried. After all, Jesus could have worried about any number of things. But instead of worrying, He teaches us to look at the flowers because they are always beautiful. And He teaches us to look at the birds because they always have food when they need it. They know how to build nests. I will grant you, spending the winter in a bird's nest is not my idea of a good time, but Jesus' point is well made.

Worrying about your financial condition does not make it any better. Worrying about your clothing does not put clothing on your body. Worrying about shelter never got you into a place of safety in the time of a storm.

It is only when worrying moves on into trusting that we can really find the answers to the problems that seem to defeat us. I know it is tough when you are looking at one can of pasta in the cupboard and wonder about the next meal.

What are we to do? I had a friend ask me the other day how you take all your burdens and worries and turn them over to God. She thought since I have my own battles and I am a pastor, I should have a great answer for her. I know her question was serious because I know about her life situations. But I did not have an answer for her then.

But I believe I have an answer for her now. Let's take Jesus' advice in Matthew 6. We should first ask God for our daily needs. That may take time to soak in as my mind aligns with God's mind. But I need to focus on what my needs really are and ask Him to help me see it like He does.

Secondly, I need to try not to worry. If there is anything I have discovered, it is that I am human. When I get something stuck in my brain, it seems like it stays there. So, what I can do is ask Him to help me not to worry. I need to ask Him to help me refocus (remember this from an earlier chapter?) on what is important. I admit that sometimes this doesn't work as well as I'd like. At night, when I am lying in bed and I hear every pop and crack of the house, it is tough. But when I am awake, I can keep my mind occupied to think on the things that help me move forward.

I can refocus and keep working to the best of my ability. I can think on good things, pray for other people, once again lay my petitions before the God who made me and understands me better than anyone else. And in so doing, I find I can get by until an answer comes!

I am not defined by what I do or by what I have. I am not a better person because I worry. I am not a better person because I have a Ford instead of a Lincoln. I am not a better person because I live in a mansion instead of a cabin.

No, I am defined by whose I am. And that will make all the difference in the world. I look to the one who loves me and provides for me. And that is ultimately what I need to know when my money is failing me.

I hope you, like me, want to be just like Jesus. I think that should be our ultimate goal. But when it comes to dealing with my finances, I would like to be just like the woman in Luke 21. Listen to Luke relate Jesus' words to us: Luke 21:2-4 "He also saw a poor widow put in two very small copper coins. (3) 'Truly I tell you,' he said, 'this poor widow has put in more than all the others. (4) All these people gave their gifts out of their wealth; but she out of her poverty put in all she had to live on.'"

I wish I could say that I had this woman's attitude about money. I am working on it. One day I hope to have the faith she exhibited. She gave all she had. She believed it was right. She knew that if she gave what she had that God would bless her with oodles of noodles. And that would be enough for her. I want it to be enough for me too!

> *An Everyday Jesus for the Everyday Life – Chapter 7*
> # When Thorns Take Over Your Bed of Roses
> *"When Your Marriage Has Problem"*

Like everybody else, my wife and I have had our fair share of issues in marriage! But whatever problems we did have, we found a way to work out. It isn't always easy because we are two people with two different backgrounds and two different upbringings. Our likes and dislikes are obvious. I am a meatloaf fanatic; she is a liver lover. She likes red; I like blue. I am probably a bit more free-spending concerning money; she likes to save for a rainy day.

But despite our differences, I could never have asked for a woman who could have loved me more in our marriage. When one of us has health problems, the other is the mother hen (or father rooster), that pushes the way through. We pray for each other, hope for the best, and love even deeper, while still finding those moments to be ourselves.

We have seen, and tried to help people through, difficult times with marriages. Like most families, our family has not been untouched by marital stresses. I am choosing, however, to leave my family out of this particular discussion. I do want to share a story with you about a couple that I loved with all my heart and a difficult time they faced. I have changed their names though you probably would never know these people.

Rob and Patti were a strong leadership couple in one of the churches that I served. He was gregarious and bright, a real hands-on farmer type. She was a great homemaker, a loving mom, a wonderful cook, and an intuitive wife because she could almost read her husband's mind in every situation. However, one night, about 9:00 p.m. or so, their world was totally and unequivocally shaken. I got the call, I don't remember now from whom, that their home was on fire. The fire department was hoping they could save it.

I did not have much pastoral experience at that point and time, although I don't know that I could do much different today. As I drove down the country road to their house, I could see the trucks and lights and the tongues of flame licking up their valuable possessions. People were milling about everywhere. The fire department tried, but it was impossible to contain the fire. It was simply too far along.

Rob was trying his best to keep an eye on things, checking with the fire department, and wandering in the smokey maze. Patti was tied to her possessions in the house. I spent most of the time with her. She seemed the most distraught. She looked at the house and in tears and agony walked away holding one picture that she had been able to grab on the way out of the burning home, a family picture. That picture was her tie to security.

Finally, Rob and Patti headed toward the home of a near-by family member. They tried to go to sleep with visions of the orange fingers grasping and dissolving everything they owned. It was, understandably, a restless night for them.

Not too many days after, Rob came to me and told me about Patti. She wasn't the same. Her world was crushed, she was depressed, and he was in tears trying to figure out what to do to help the situation. I didn't have any answers. I spoke with her, but she was lost in the rubble of her life. It did not take very long until Rob and Patti divorced. Rob tried to do everything he could. But it seemed it was just too late to make a difference. Heartbroken, Rob left his leadership role in the church. Patti went her way. Another marriage dissolved.

Since then, they have both remarried, but I have not seen either of them for several years.

Divorce is a devastating nightmare that rears its ugly head still today. Men and women become confused about the glue that stuck them together in the beginning and how to make it hold when trying times come up! It is a hard thing to deal with!

I wish that I could give you book, chapter, and verse, of a scripture that would tell you where you could go to find the answer to deal with problems in marriages, especially like this one. If there were only some magical incantation that you could speak that would bring your lost love back to you. If we could only wish for a miracle to make everything just like it was back in those early days of marriage, so things don't hurt.

While I can't do that, maybe I can give you something to lean on while you are dealing with a heart break like this. Let's look at a scripture and keep your Bible open there if you will because we will be right back to this chapter. Here in Matthew 19:8 Jesus replied, "Moses permitted you to divorce your wives because your hearts were hard. But it was not this way from the beginning."

According to Strong's Analytical Concordance, the phrase "hard of heart" means having a destitution of perception. In other words, husbands were divorcing their wives because they could no longer see the value in the relationship. Divorce happened because men could not keep their minds in focus on the wife of their youth. Jesus comments that while divorce was allowed, that wasn't the way God wanted it. Moral consequence has never changed.

As I was writing this chapter, a rain storm came up. The lightning was brilliant and somewhat dangerous. The thunder was loud. The rain was hard, and the wind blew a bit. It was nice because we have not had any rain around here in a while.

As I was trying to work through this passage in my mind, God led me outside to watch the storm from the church porch. I certainly did not want to go out in it. There was danger of being struck by lightning and I did not have an umbrella to keep dry. Had I gone out in it, I would have been at the mercy of the storm.

If you are the innocent victim in a divorce, realize that the hardness of the spouse's heart is much like the storm. There may not be much you can do about it. What you can do is what I did in protecting myself from the storm: get yourself into a safe place, away from danger. Ride out the rough moments as best you can until the storm subsides. Then you can continue with your life, in whatever form that may be. And in trying to maintain your sanity in this storm you didn't want or cause, you can plant in your mind the words of Peter in I Peter 5:7: "Cast all your anxiety on him because he cares for you." When it seems that special person no longer cares, bring that anxiousness to Jesus, and let Him do what He wants to do. You cannot fathom what the possibilities are!

But something else you might think about, especially if you are contemplating marriage, is divorce proofing your marriage. We are going to look at Matthew 19 again, but some different verses.

Before we get to that, though, let me encourage you to get the word divorce out of your vocabulary, even before you think about marriage. My wife and I have a standing joke between us that we often relate to other people. We never talk about divorce. Murder yes, but never divorce. Of course, we think it is hilarious! And people politely laugh with us, but it is certainly worth thinking about. In your relationship, if you never think about divorce being an option, then it never will be. Replace that thought with a mindset of a successful marriage.

Do you want a successful marriage? Here are three things to have clear in your mind, and in your future mate's mind, before you walk the aisle of holy matrimony, courtesy of Matthew.

First, let us clearly identify the purpose of marriage. We see a sneak peek of that in Matthew 19:4, "Haven't you read," he replied, "that at the beginning the Creator 'made them male and female.'" Marriage was designed by God in the beginning to be between a man and a woman. That is simply what the Bible says! This seems to me to be most important because the differences in gender fulfill God's plan to procreate, to bring live offspring to the face of the earth.
God ceased creating people and charged the first man and woman, and succeeding generations, to populate the earth. This is the only way it can be realistically done.

Then, secondly, let us clearly understand that God's demonstration of His love for the church exemplifies a part of the husband and wife relationship. A husband who leads his home with love like Jesus and who has respect for the needs of his wife, will be successful. Sometimes my family asks me why I encourage my wife to take the time and resources to be with her family. I know it is important to her. And if it is important to her, it is important to me. This is not necessarily a teaching of Jesus in this passage, but it is a truth that I have discovered. I feel many men might be missing a blessing by not letting their wives grow as they need to. Check out Ephesians 5:22ff for further understanding of God's way

Finally, clearly believe that the words of Jesus in Matthew 19:5ff show us a few things that truly need to be in place to make marriage a success. Let's take a look.

This scripture, first, helps us see that the judge or minister says the words but God is the one who does the joining together. I don't think this suggests that all marriages are made in heaven and that you can only find that one certain mate who will make your life whole. But I am convinced that this does say that God's gift of marriage is to provide hope and fulfillment in their lives. When a marriage commitment is made, this scripture suggests that the marriage is then sealed by God and therefore a Holy Union, unlike any other.

Consider as a part of this important concept that not everyone has the gift of marriage. Not everyone is meant to be married. Matthew 19:11 seems to hint at this: "Jesus replied, 'Not everyone can accept this word, but only those to whom it has been given.'" Some will be able to serve God better if they are not in the marriage relationship because their time will be more directed toward God. A marriage relationship is neither good or bad. Being married or not is a gift God has given you.

Secondly, look at Matthew 19:6 "So they are no longer two, but one flesh. Therefore what God has joined together, let no one separate." Consider with me what it means to say that "God has joined together…"

As a result of working on this book, I think that I shall give a bottle of glue to every couple I perform a wedding for. And then I will read the scripture, "What God has joined together," because the word picture behind this is that God "glues" together. Some marriages seem to be bonded in super glue while others seem linked by only weak paste. The glue that God is using is designed to permanently stick a man and woman together as long as they both shall live. The only solvent that can pull this glue apart is the solvent that the woman and the man use in an ill-planned desire to break the bond that God has established. If you are in the process of thinking about marriage, think about the fact that when you tie the knot, God's glue will hold the bond. Nothing will be able to break that bond except the two of you. Other things may tug on you, but you alone make the choice about how your marriage will work.

Thirdly, understand what divorce is. Jesus puts it clearly in this passage of scripture from Matthew 19:9, "I tell you that anyone who divorces his wife, except for sexual immorality, and marries another woman commits adultery." In another of Jesus' sayings, we see that the woman who is divorced is also made an adulteress, even if she had nothing to do with the situation at hand.

The culture of Jesus' day was usually about the men leaving their wives. Wives could be divorced for many reasons, such as the following: Talking to men not of family, spinning in the street, wearing her hair unbound, serving him food that was not tithed, being a scolding woman (loud enough to be heard outside of the house) and more.[7]

Today, it is not just men's hearts who get hard but also women's. That does not make divorce any more pleasing to God. It is truly a sad thing to see so much hatred and animosity exist in a relationship that was designed to be successful, no matter how the whole thing got started!

The only legitimate grounds for the divorce is sexual immorality. And that is not what God really wants. He just knows that people's hearts get hard.

Let me ask you to make sure that if you are planning nuptials that you do so with the image of being under God's plan, as long as you both shall live. It will be rewarding and fruitful if you do so.

You may be a meatloaf fanatic and your spouse a liver lover. You may like different colors and you may have different money habits. A time will come when your bed of roses becomes uncomfortable with some thorns that emerge. If you find that this is true for you, let these insights help you. No one can guarantee you a life of no thorns, but if you do it God's way, you will find no other way does it better.

> An Everyday Jesus for the Everyday Life – Chapter 8
> ## Sometimes I Forget That!
> *"When Worldly Morality Challenges Us"*

In the 1960's, a "Yellow Submarine" made its way across the Atlantic Ocean to the theaters and stages of America. Four funny looking guys named Ringo, Paul, George, and John, made their mark on American television and in the hearts of many American youth. Sporting shaggy hair-does and an unorthodox sound in music, the Beatles set the standard for a new generation. Many groups would develop their own styles of this new sound.

About this same time, a young man from Memphis, Tennessee, was beginning to swing his hips and strum out a new sound that would also help define that generation. Elvis Presley began to croon "Blue Suede Shoes" and "You Ain't Nothin' But a Hound Dog". His style of music and delivery drove the young women insane.

We are now more than 50 years from the time these people started being movers and shakers in the music industry. Yet their names are still known by about everyone living today. Some love them. Some hate them. But everybody knows them.

My parents were outspoken about their feelings. Many people of their generation spoke out also. They considered the music, the hair styles, and antics of these rock stars to be immoral. I seem to recall many people saying that this music would be the "ruination" of the nation! This music was seen by many as a moral issue.

You can agree or disagree with the opinions people expressed. I will feel free to say, however, that most every generation questions the morality of the music of the next generation. I wondered about the music of my children. They question the music of their children. And more than likely they will question the music of their children.

From magazines to television shows, from literature to internet web sites, and from the ethics of medicine to the style of math taught in schools, most everybody has an opinion as to its taste and morality. The lines seem firmly drawn.

I am not a fan of tattoos and I realize that many serious-minded people stand firmly against them as a violation of the Old Testament. Yet there is a market for tattoos for people of faith that demonstrate their love for Jesus.

I did observe, this week, a unique tattoo that made me scratch my head. At the local grocery store, a single mom and her small daughter were talking to the clerk, finishing up their order. It was difficult, however, to miss the "sleeve", or arm-length tattoo, that mom wore. Featured prominently on her arm was the figure of a naked woman. I have seen tattoos like that on men, but I confess I have never seen a woman wearing a tattoo of a naked woman. Many things have changed in the society in which we live and I am sure many things will continue to change. The morality of those changes will be questioned by people of faith around our world. The debate will continue to be what is culture verses what is immoral!

It is highly unlikely that a miracle will blanket the world that will make each person in each generation see things the same way. Because that is true, a standard is needed to determine what really is a moral issue and what really is a cultural issue. I know of no better place to find this information than in the words of the everyday Savior for the everyday life! With your permission, I would like to present three teachings of Jesus that will help us decide the whether it is culture or whether it is a moral issue.

The first teaching that I would like to share is more an observation of what Jesus did than what Jesus taught. I feel it is important to understand this because Jesus never seemed to say, "Do what I say, don't do as I do!" Jesus was unique in teaching because He could perfectly demonstrate. Unlike the pro basketball player of a few years ago who declared that kids shouldn't watch him because he would refuse to be a role model for them, Jesus lived out everything He taught.

The most revealing thing in Jesus' ministry, and living out His teaching, is that Jesus could sit with sinners and not sin. He could talk to tax collectors, prostitutes, thieves, murderers, and self-righteous religious people and never join them in their sin. He showed it was possible to live out the good news and share the good news, but not join in the sin to do it.

I had been visiting with a church family and they had been sharing the needs of their neighbor. So one evening, about 7:00 or so, I knocked on his door hoping to get acquainted. I could see through the screen door that he was sitting down in front of the TV. He did not seem to be occupied otherwise and was happy to let me come in and chat. What I had not seen in his hand was the bottle of beer. In a friendly and jovial manner he asked, "Preacher, would you like a beer!" I politely declined because I felt it was not correct for me as a Christian to drink alcohol, though I know many do and enjoy it. I felt most comfortable getting acquainted and speaking of Christ without the bottle in my hand.

Perhaps a preacher friend of mine took the whole issue one step further when he told me about a Bible study he was conducting in a tavern not far from his house. He made it clear that he did not drink, but he did conduct a study where he introduced Jesus to people in the tavern. His hope was that he could visit the other tavern in town and do the same thing.

My point is not to get you to go into the taverns to do Bible studies. My concern, however, is that sometimes we strive to be so careful to dot our spiritual i's and cross our spiritual t's that we don't get to where the sinners are. It has also been my observation that it is rare for a sinner to just stumble into a church. Actively reaching out to people is important and must be done without diminishing the witness we have for Jesus. I look for ways to meet them on their turf yet help people to realize I am not selling out my faith, only hoping to multiply it or give them something that they need.

So, when I am dealing with an issue of morality, I need to ask myself the question, does this compromise the way my faith will be seen by other people. While there are always Pharisees who will be critical of what we do when they don't like it, moral or just cultural, we are encouraged to always set the best example for Christ and ignore such judgements, just as Jesus did.

The second thing that Jesus shows us is that there is never a proper place in the life of a Christian for adultery and other sexual sin. These seem not to ever be cultural issues, that it seems the culture keeps forcing them upon us. For some informational reading, check out Romans 1:18-32. In this scripture, Paul spells out how rejection of God has led to open sexual sin with the opposite sex, then to homosexuality, and finally to the giving over to a depraved mind. In the day and age in which this book is being written, it is fairly easy to see how this trail is being followed by the world.

Jesus echoes these thoughts in His teachings anyway, so to stay true to our theme for seeing the Everyday Jesus for the Everyday life, let us see what He has to say. We might see that His words have a certain unpleasant bite to both the world and believers who have believed the world.

In John 8, Jesus has encountered a very scared young woman. She has been dragged before the crowd by the Pharisees. If she was taken in the act of adultery, she was probably scantily clad and embarrassed to death as she stood before the crowd, and you can be sure there was a crowd as the Pharisees wanted to trap Jesus in the presence of many witnesses.

This young woman was now regretting her moment of weakness. She saw she was to be the helpless pawn in the war now taking place.

After Jesus had put the self-righteous Pharisees in their place, He turned His attention to the scared young woman. What would Jesus do? The Pharisees were right. Adultery was to be punished by stoning. What was on this Jesus' mind the woman could not tell, but she did have hope as she looked at Him.

What Jesus knew was the Pharisees had not bothered to bring the man who committed adultery. Jesus could do nothing for the man, but He could for the woman. In verse 11, the great Rabbi of God proclaimed he would not condemn the woman. He did tell her to leave her life of sin. He did not water down the sin; but He loved and dealt as only He could!

In Matthew 5:7, Jesus explicitly condemns adultery to the point that He explains that even giving continuing thought to adultery was itself adultery. Lust was something that Jesus could not abide. And that is a tough pill for many to swallow when it seems to interfere with their happiness!

In Matthew, and again in Luke, Jesus uses Sodom and Gomorrah as an illustration of things God considered wicked. Jesus never, ever, approved of homosexuality as an alternate lifestyle. Again, because the issue has become so rampant, we tend to water down such issues. And honestly, sometimes our situation must be like Jesus who sat with the sinners and taught them but did not share in their sin.

If the moral issue of the day that is put in front of you involves some sort of sexual sin, please be sure that this is an issue of morality and not an issue of culture. Satan is still trying to sell us a bill of goods.

The third teaching that Jesus gives us when there is no miracle to challenge the possible moral issue that we face, is that which is really the premise for the whole Bible, for everything we need to know about our relationship with God. This is found in Mark 12:30-31, "Love the Lord your God with all your heart and with all your soul and with all your mind and with all your strength.' (31) The second is this: 'Love your neighbor as yourself.' There is no commandment greater than these."

Let us suppose that you are trying to decide that you want to skip out on a day of work, or in the case of students, a day of school. You know the system. You only have to call in and say you are sick and then go spend the afternoon at the ball park for the day game of your local team. You justify this to yourself by saying that everybody does it once in a while. That it is no big deal. And so, you make plans to buy the tickets so you can go. You call in, you lie, and you do what you want to do. It doesn't hurt anybody!

But you say that you love God with all your heart, soul, and mind. And you love your neighbor as yourself. Do you? You probably just lied to your boss, which is certainly against God's teaching and you have not loved your neighbor as yourself because you would cheat the boss. Even though everybody does it, a cultural issue, it is certainly not right morally because you have violated two of the greatest commands in existence.

Everybody does drugs. Everybody cheats on their spouse. Everybody takes advantage of things at work. Everybody oversleeps and ignores church. Everybody does everything without thinking about how that is going to harm or even destroy a relationship with God and with others. Prayer and Bible reading really doesn't matter? I hope you will consider again what the world is throwing at us. I suppose the list could be endless when it comes to seeking justification for doing the wrongs and making them look right. If it hurts your relationship with God and others, there are moral issues involved.

He was hard to miss. His red checked shirt barely buttoned in several places. I never figured out why he wore the black lanyard around his neck. His pockets looked a lot like mine, stuffed with pens and little note books, and probably more little treasures to him than I could imagine. An old workman's cap was pulled down over his face and his silver hair hung out underneath of it, slightly curled from the wear and tear of the day. The pants were dirty and rumpled and an old belt reached around his middle.

His smile was a brilliant one, an exact contrast to the rest of his appearance, though it seemed to gleam along with the sparkle in his eye. He looked mostly homeless to me, but everybody in the fast food restaurant knew him and spoke to him. He was a regular Saturday visitor for belly bombers!

We struck up a conversation while we both were waiting on our food. He commented that it was a nice day. I said that yes it was and the Lord had given us a good one. He made a comment that totally surprised me because it seemed his attention was fixed holding his cup under the soda dispenser. I can hear his comment, filtered slightly by his small moustache, "Yes it is! Sometimes I forget that." "Sometimes I forget that!"

How often it is true that we criticize someone's choice of music or of reading material? "Why, they like that music. How can a Christian like that?" "I don't care for that genre of reading. It seems so silly. God wouldn't like that!"

Sometimes we use those statements to judge. Sometimes we speak them in ignorance. Usually we speak them without God's kind of love. And frequently we speak these words because we just don't care about looking with God's eyes! Sometimes we don't really think about "cultural" or "moral". Instead of judging others, we need to pray for them to see God's way.

Let us, then, decide today that we will start seeking morality decisions about our own issues. I will look at how I can be with sinners, but still serve without becoming like them. I will be honest and realize that if adultery is ever the problem, maintaining morality is always the answer. And if it hurts my relationship with God, I have to let it go. It is a Biblical standard I must apply!

I need to make sure that I am applying these principles carefully. I need to make sure that I am doing what God wants. Because sometimes, I forget that!

> *An Everyday Jesus for the Everyday Life – Chapter 9*
> # You Talked My Leg Off
> *"When Our Bodies Let Us Down"*

"I just don't know why the Lord is keeping me here. I am ready to go home!" Mary was 100 years young. Her health had been deteriorating for many years. Her arthritis was so bad she was more than miserable. From her perspective there was no reason for her to be on the face of this earth. She loved the Lord and she knew where she was going when her final breath was drawn. She had always been a hard worker, but Mary now could not do anything. People helped her with the simplest day to day tasks. It gnawed at her. She felt helpless and useless and I am not sure which one she thought was worse.

We were all very sensitive to Mary's plight because we knew many people who had asked the same question. Our answer to her was always the same, "You are being a great Christian example and an encouragement to people." I am not sure the answer ever made her happy. But neither did any of us lie to Mary. People were always astounded when they saw her sitting in church, right up to the end, and found out she was 100 years old. Her faith was rock solid and she kept her convictions true to the end, even if her convictions ruffled a few feathers. Mary had a great testimony and even now, several years after passing, her influence is still being felt in many people's lives.

Old age is just one of the ways our bodies let us down. I have a very good friend who was a tremendous worker for the kingdom. She loved kids and worked with children/youth of any age. Unfortunately, due to complications from a surgery, she lost part of her leg. After more than a year, she is working hard to do what she did before sporting a prosthetic leg. She always kept a goal in mind and sought to achieve it. She was an avid golfer and even had a golf picture on the material surrounding the prosthesis to remind herself what she wanted to strive for.

For some of us, unexpected health challenges are an issue. Just about the time I chose to start laying out the ground work for this book, I received word that I was going to be facing a battle with prostate cancer. After the myriad of tests and procedures, I will soon begin radiation treatment for it, a treatment that will take half a day of about 9 weeks' worth of days. Added to this is the excitement and challenge of a church that God has blessed and is beginning to grow in His name after many years of sitting silent. My wish through this whole time has been that God would be glorified. And that is still my wish. But in those silent and alone moments, Satan's minions sometimes tempt me to be worried. And sometimes it is easy to forget the blessings that come even though our bodies begin to let us down.

You can add the issues you know. Perhaps you are dealing with a disease that robs the movement of your body. Something in your digestive system no longer works as it is supposed to. Maybe you have found yourself forgetting where you are going or how to get there. Maybe it seems like you have been in the hospital a lot lately. All these things seem to stand in the way of you being the servant that you so long to be. And, like my friend Mary, you find yourself helpless or useless and you are not sure which is worse!

The bad news is that some of these things are not going to change easily, or maybe not at all. The good news is that there are some great people of faith in the Bible who did not find a miraculous answer for the problems that they faced and you can take hope in what happened with them.

Timothy, the friend of Paul, was challenged to take a little wine for his stomach sake. There was no miracle for him. The Apostle Paul said that he implored God to take away his personal thorn in the flesh, whatever that happened to be. Yet he saw that thorn helped him maintain his ability to serve and so he gladly went without a miracle but with the hope of God tucked in his heart.

If you and I could sit down over a cup of coffee and talk about the challenges that face your body and my body, I would strongly encourage you to have Paul's attitude. There might well be no miracle for what you have. In fact, the road to treatment, or the only road in front of you, might not involve a miracle. But despite that fact, you can go a long way when the words of Jesus are tucked in your heart. The words are so precious, and so sweet, and so powerful, that they can help you move through the worst of times to have the greatest hope.

If you would allow me, I'd like to point out some things from Matthew 8. And while you are grabbing a Bible and getting ready to think about what is in there, I would like to point out something I discovered about having my body fail me. It was something my friend who was dealing with old age also discovered! When you have some sort of an issue where your body lets you down, you tend to encounter people you have not encountered before. And these become people with whom you can share in some way about Jesus.

I was required to have a bone scan upon the cancer diagnosis. I went to the hospital to prepare for the test by receiving an injection of radioactive material. Then I would return two hours later to lay under the "Geiger counter", if you will, to have the test run.

The lady who did the test was absolutely one of the nicest people I ever met. In conversation, I was telling her about a book I had read on facing difficulties in life and I shared with her my dream of doing this book. She listened appreciably. She shared a particular family issue she was facing and how helpful something like this could be.

We parted ways for the two hours so the dye could do its job. I had scrambled eggs, bacon, and waffles. She had time to think. When I returned she told me that she had been thinking a lot about the book I read and the book I was writing. She expressed to me how much something like that would be of help to her. We chatted a bit more and then I laid on the table to have the test. In just a few moments the test was done. She explained to me what the scanners were showing and why what we had just done was so important.

As the discussion was over, she walked to the door and started to open it. But I think God had another idea in mind. Very quickly, I received the thought to offer prayer. When I did offer it, she was immediately touched and at peace. I was thrilled to see what was happening in her life and what God could do. We corresponded by email once, but like Philip leaving the Ethiopian Eunuch, our paths have not crossed. However, we were both blessed in what the Lord had allowed to happen that morning.

In the course of my treatment, I have had other chances to pray and to share. I hope I will be an instrument in the hands of God to touch the lives of as many people as He allows into my path. Mary had the opportunity to touch lives. My friend with the prosthesis had the opportunity to touch lives. And as much as it is likely you will face some challenge of this sort, I pray that you will be ready to touch those lives also.

Another observation about times when our bodies let us down came from a very insightful young lady whose advice and encouragement I greatly admire. Her comment to me was that when we face these times, we are forced to move out of our comfort zone. And when we do that, we are more able to see the rough edges knocked off. In turn, since Jesus is molding those edge, He can help us be more like Him.

I readily confess that I like sitting in my comfort zone. I don't have to change there. It is less stressful that way. It is also very likely that in that zone, I am far from being what Jesus wants me to be. In evidence of that, look how Jesus buffed and polished the lives of the 12 men who traveled with Him. They quit being fishermen and became fishers of men because of the work Jesus did through walking on water and preaching and serving without taking the necessities along. Yes, they saw miracles, but ultimately it was the words of that Savior that changed and shined their hearts for all eternity. It was an amazing transformation, one that challenges us today.

I love Matthew chapter 8. In that chapter, in the first verses, Jesus performs healings on four different people. I can hear your objection--"but this involves miracles that Jesus did". I don't dispute it or deny it. But I asked you if in such circumstances you would join me in looking past the miracle. In doing so I knew that you would see some wonderful words.

As I look at this, I realize that Jesus had an expectation for the leper. The words from Matthew 8:4 are: "See that you don't tell anyone. But go, show yourself to the priest and offer the gift Moses commanded, as a testimony to them." We can only guess, my opinion anyway, that Jesus did not want His ministry made to be a circus sideshow. What he was asking of the leper was obedience to the His words which reflected the words of God's Old Testament law.

Obedience is a huge word when our bodies let us down! If the problem we have is one of health that is compromised by an activity we perform, it is important for us to examine how well we are obeying that which can help us be healthy.

An alcoholic, or someone with a condition compromised by alcohol, would be counseled to leave the alcoholic drink alone. The smoker possibly facing a cancer or other issue, knows the importance of leaving the cigarettes out of his life. The person who is dealing with issues of age, realizes, or will realize, the need to stop climbing ladders, driving the vehicle, or other activities that might be risky based on their stage of life. A person who must take certain medicines to maintain health, may not wish to take them, but must if they choose to enjoy the blessing of life.

Obedience can be very hard sometimes. We are people who have a choice and who enjoy freewill. We are people who are used to being independent. Often it is very difficult to make the change. But obedience is important.

Obedience to Jesus and His way remains important no matter what we are doing. If I were to lose the use of an arm, that in no way gives me permission to violate or ignore God's law just because something has happened in my life. As

I get older and more frustrated, I am not relieved of the command to use God's name wisely. Because I am only able to sit in a rocking chair, I am not excused from knowing Jesus Christ as my Savior and doing my best to serve Him and believe in Him and the Salvation He brings.

Obedience is important! May we always obey, no matter what our bodies are robbing us of the ability to do.

In Matthew 8, we also read about the Centurion who had a servant who was very sick. When you read the passage, you see Jesus' question to the Centurion, "Shall I come and heal him?" (vs. 7) But in verse 8, we see the heart of the Centurion, the military leader over a group of 100 men. He says, "Lord, I do not deserve to have you come under my roof. But just say the word, and my servant will be healed." The Centurion had a great deal of faith in what Jesus could do. The centurion knew that Jesus could speak the words and things would happen. That is what he banked on here. He was NOT disappointed! Jesus did the very thing based on the man's faith.

How about you? What kind of faith do you have? You might be saying to me, "Oh, Randy, I have faith that Jesus will heal me!" I truly hope He does if you offer that prayer. But understand many times it does not work that way and it has nothing to do with your faith. He just chooses not to heal you of a specific need for his purpose. And that is ok because God obviously has something bigger and better in mind than we can imagine.

But we do come back to the aspect of trusting Jesus to be with us when we face those trials in life, whatever they might be. Does Jesus leave us because we are aged? Or does Jesus leave us because we have cancer? Or does Jesus leave us because we get dementia. The answer is always a resounding NO! He did not say in vain, "I am with you always, even unto the end of the age." May we always be confident in that fact.

I only want to mention the last two miracles. One was Jesus healing Peter's mother-in-law and the other was Jesus healing the multitudes. You can follow up on this in Matthew 8:14-17 if you would like. The restoration of Peter's mother-in-law was obviously complete as she got up and went about taking care of the house and the needs of the house. The multitudes were healed that day of the demons that possessed them. And what a marvelous time it must have been as Jesus sent the minions of Satan on their way.

But these last two healings point to a very important lesson and that is why Jesus did the healings. It was not to glorify Himself or any man. It was to be the fulfillment of the greatest scripture of hope every recorded from Isaiah 53:4, "Surely he took up our pain and bore our suffering," (NIV)

I don't know why you undergo the sufferings you do! I don't know why your body is not acting like it used to, except for age of course. But know this, Jesus is helping you bear the burdens that you face, and ultimately, He understands because He helped you carry them when you think you could do no more. And that is a wonderful hope!

You never got to meet Sarah. She was a delightful lady. Sarah loved the Lord and people knew it. She was fun at parties because she knew how to make people laugh. She knew how to steal a hot dog or hide a piece of pie and have everybody in stitches. Sarah did not have an easy life. She had the responsibility of raising several grandchildren. Toward the end of her days, Sarah developed a circulation problem in her leg and after several different delays, finally had that leg amputated. Not even that would get Sarah down. She kept on bringing joy to people. Yes, she had her silent moments when things happened that were hard for her to deal with. But she always remained faithful and trusted in God, even with the worries of her situation.

One Sunday morning as I was preaching, I looked back to where Sarah was sitting and I noticed a funny look came over her face. Nothing seemed to be terribly wrong except her scooting around and fidgeting a bit more than normal, so I continued with my message. After the service was over, I asked Sarah what happened. And this what she said, in a low voice, "Preacher while you were speaking this morning, my artificial leg came off. It didn't really bother me, but I was trying to get it put back into place. I finally did, but it was a terrible chore."

That explanation seemed good enough for me. She turned around to leave, as did I. But Sarah suddenly stopped and said, "Preacher, you know, I have never had a preacher talk my leg off in church!"

Sarah has gone on to be with the Lord. She continued to be a great example of Christian faith, just like the examples we talked about. While her body failed her, the Lord never did. Neither did Sarah fail the Lord. And, I never talked anybody else's leg off!

An Everyday Jesus for the Everyday Life – Chapter 10
The Expected Unexpected
"When Death Surprises Us"

Prologue: *The sun was shining. The birds were singing. It was an ideal day. What problem could possibly come up?*

The resident of a brown tile house, very close to the church building where I served as minister, was in my sights that day. So far, everyone else seemed warm and open and anxious to speak with me. Being the only preacher in town, preaching at the only church in town, I hoped to connect and hopefully help them all walk with Jesus.

Approaching the simple tile house, I noted the concrete sidewalk was stained with weather and with age. The steps that led up to the porch leaned backward almost as if poured that way. Cracks filled the gray painted concrete floor of the porch. The screen door had loose and ripped screens with an ancient heavy door behind it.

I knocked. Someone bustled about inside but seemed not to hear the door. I knocked again, much more vigorously. Finally, after a small eternity, a woman, probably in her 30's, came to the door. As I started to introduce myself, her expression changed. Anger filled her face and her vehement tone left no room for doubt about the emotion that she felt.

"Oh, I know who you are," she said. "And I don't want to talk to you!!!" And with that the heavy door slammed shut. The force of that ancient door slamming shut pushed a breeze through the screen that seemed to smack me in the face. It didn't make sense. I had never met the lady before. What had caused such an angry outburst? I went away, vowing never to step foot on that porch again! Next time, I thought, she just might have a gun.

The Hebrew writer speaks a great truth. Hebrews 9:27 reminds us, "...people are destined to die once, and after that to face judgment." It is a difficult fact for us to face. But it is true that 100 out of 100 people will die, unless the Lord should come first.

Satan understood exactly how mankind thinks. Job 2:4 reminds us of these words, "'Skin for skin!' Satan replied. 'A man will give all he has for his own life.'" We will fight viciously to stay alive. We struggle with the ravages of age. We spend millions of dollars to make ourselves look young. We take pills to help us live longer. We exercise and have skin tucks, all to make us think that youth and life are eternal. And we even buy life insurance, sure that we won't need it until sometime WAY down the road. And, in fact, it is often sold to us with that thought in mind. Eve even relied on that longevity when Satan tricked her in Genesis 3 convincing her that she did not need to worry about death because of sin.

Again, we return to Hebrews 9:7. We are destined to die once and then we can anticipate standing before God. It will happen.

No miracle is going to change it. So, what can I learn about living and dying that can add a new dimension to my life? I don't know of any other place to look that is better than John 11. In this text, Lazarus has died, but Jesus has waited. His plan was to ultimately resurrect Lazarus after 4 days in the tomb. Yes, this would be a miracle but some very important teachings come to light from the everyday side of Jesus, the side that teaches us the things we need to know to get us through life successfully, even in the face of death. I am convinced that there are some great teachings that the everyday Jesus shares that will help us prepare for the time our lives end.

When you are contemplating your death, or the death of someone close to you, the first truth I would have you grab onto is from John 11:35, the shortest verse in the Bible, a verse I usually try to bring out in a funeral service.

"Jesus wept" you say? That is exactly right. The fact is that Jesus cared about Mary and Martha and Lazarus and everybody around the tomb. If you stop and consider that Jesus knew what was going to happen, surely the weeping was not because of grief and sorrow in Jesus' mind. He knew Lazarus would be right back! John 11:33 shows that Mary was weeping as were the people there. Jesus was moved with emotion for and with those who were present.

Some people seem to have their only image of God as sitting up in heaven looking for people to cast lightning bolts down upon. He is pictured as a punisher, which might be seen in the Old Testament. That's not our Jesus.

I, also, find no reason to believe that Jesus cares any less about the situations in which we find ourselves than He did about Mary and Martha. I Peter reminds us, in fact, that we can cast our cares upon Him. Here is a new picture of God, a picture of a God who cares, and who, in form of Jesus, sat with and wept with people who were hurting. It is the picture of the Good Shepherd who goes after the sheep, at all costs. It is a picture of the dying form of the Savior Himself being the sacrifice to change the lives of people everywhere, loving so much He gave Himself up for us, the sheep of His pasture. It is a picture you can stake your life on!

Here is another thought from Jesus that is so vital as we consider life and death and our perspective of death. John

11:40 records, "Then Jesus said, 'Did I not tell you that if you believe, you will see the glory of God?'"

In my years of doing funerals, I don't think I ever remember anybody ever saying that they saw the glory of God in death. Oh, people commented that their loved one was going to heaven. And the loved one was in a better place. In fact, I have heard many statements made about heaven. But seeing some sort of glory that helped the kingdom of God really was nothing I could ever remember.

Our 20/20 hindsight helps us to see that God was going to be glorified when Lazarus came back to life. People would be so excited. The thrill and exhilaration of the returning loved one would be something that would live in their hearts forever. Here was a great miracle. Here was someone who could do a great miracle! Here was one who had been dead for 4 days. It just did not happen that people die and come back to life after 4 days. The mood would be ecstatic!

Our 20/20 hindsight also helps us to see that Martha, practical and hardworking Martha, hardly could have believed such a thing was possible. But she did after Jesus called to Lazarus and the dead man came out of the tomb still wrapped in the burial cloth. After the wraps came off, oh, yes, God was glorified. John 11:45 tells us that this marvelous miracle brought many to believe in whom Jesus was. Even the skeptics said that what was happening was a marvelous sign and that Jesus was doing it. The faith of the believing grew; the hatred of the enemies grew worse!

What would our lives be like when death darkens our door, or the door of a loved one, if we could somehow ask God to turn this whole thing around to glorify Him? What if we, as Christian families, made sure that when loved ones die, the service becomes a time to praise God's work in the life of the deceased as well as to give honor to the one who has passed, bringing closure to the lives of those who remain? In lieu of a miracle, what could be better?

If I could ask you to consider one other thing, it would be the message brought to light in another part of John 11, especially verses 23-26: "Jesus said to her, 'Your brother will rise again.' (24) Martha answered, 'I know he will rise again in the resurrection at the last day.' (25) Jesus said to her, 'I am the resurrection and the life. The one who believes in me will live, even though they die; (26) and whoever lives by believing in me will never die. Do you believe this?'" (NIV)

I am convinced that in this scripture the raising of Lazarus is the convincing miracle to show the truth about who Jesus is. His promise about Lazarus was that Lazarus would live again. In making this miracle happen, the promise is made to all succeeding generations that living again in a special place, heaven, is possible because Jesus is the one who made it all possible through His death on the cross. We are part of the succeeding generations. I believe I can stake my life on it. Sure, it takes a little bit of faith, trusting in what we don't see, but that does not negate the promises. It just makes us dig a little harder to trust and when we do, we wonder why we ever doubted the thought of new life to begin with.

I unashamedly close out this little devotion by asking you to at least consider what I considered in my youth, that Jesus is real, that He died for you, that He loves you, and He wants to take you home at the end of time. Please don't just laugh it off or toss the thought aside without considering what it means if what Jesus says is true.

As I return to the story told in the prologue, I hope you will see how all the pieces I have just spoken of come together. Jump ahead in time about 2 years and allow me to finish my story.

My mother had been sick with a serious genetic blood disease most all of her life. That disease was called HHT (Hereditary Hemorrhagic Telangiectasia if you like to know the big name). It is a blood disease that affects the vessels and makes them brittle and easily ruptured. It was, and is, a fatal disease. On March 1, one week before my mother's 44th birthday, her aorta ruptured and she passed away. With today's medicine, a repair could have been made but at the time there was no fix for the problem. I knew the time of mom's death would come, but like so many people, I did not expect that the visit in the hospital would be the last time that I saw my mother living.

On the night my mother passed away, I had been out broadcasting a basketball game for the local radio station. After the hour drive back home, I was not expecting to meet Bill, the station operator that night, on the sidewalk outside the studio. He started out in his very humble way, trying to figure out how to pass the news on to his friend. And he did, with all the love and compassion one person could bring to another. I went back to my room. In the darkness of the night and at the lateness of the hour, I sobbed myself to sleep.

Being a college student at the time, I spoke to the school leaders the next day, arranged missing my classes, and headed the two-and-a-half-hour drive back to our small town. Arrangements were made and the services planned, including the request for the organist to play what I believe was my mother's favorite song, "Sheltered in the Arms of God". As I was also preaching at the church in the small town mentioned in the prologue, only about 10 miles from my home town, it was necessary to arrange a Sunday off to be with my family in our home church. We were even blessed to have my uncle from another state, fly in to share in the funeral with the family. It was a memorable time. And I believe God was glorified in the service.

I wasn't happy that my mother died, oh no! But I had and have fond memories of the way God worked through my beautiful almost 44-year-old mother. She had taught me to teach 4-year olds! She had cried with me when I went to Bible college and bravely hid her tears when she and dad left me in the college dorm, a very uncertain freshman, seeking what God wanted. And I am confident that her prayers got me through the rough days of that very first year in college. No, I wasn't happy that my mother died, but I was so blessed with the heritage she gave me. How could I be critical of what had happened, when God called her home, no longer suffering from a tortuous medical condition?

With the services now passed and the funeral now over, it was time to get back to living. I went back to college and the next week returned to the pulpit of my small-town church, eager to share the legacy my mother left in me and the hope of Christ I had learned.

Jump ahead about 1 month. Our church is in a week-long revival meeting with a professor from my Bible college leading the preaching. Attendance was good at the meeting but no one had accepted Christ during the week. On the last day, on that Friday afternoon, the evangelist and I were out making some door-to-door calls. We walked by the brown tile house. He asked me who lived there. I had since found out the woman's name was Patti. I explained the previous encounter a couple of years before. I told him the lady did not want any connection, I didn't know why, and let's go on down the road. He stopped me square in my tracks and said, "Let's go visit. The worst she can do is slam the door in our faces again." Me, I had a vision of a .22 rifle in the hands of an angry woman!

We made our way up the old weathered side walk. Age had been no kinder to it. Together we climbed up the leaning steps and walked across the crack in the concrete porch floor. The guest evangelist knocked on the door.

Patti opened the door and saw who it was. Safe so far, no gun barrel in sight! With a rather sheepish look on her face, she opened the door and invited us in to sit down. She turned away for a moment; my heart was pounding. And then Patti began to speak. I can't remember each word exactly, but I will try to be as accurate as I remember.

"Randy, when you were here last time, I was not very kind to you!" I agreed silently with that observation. "But when you stopped at my door, I had just received word that my parents were killed in a car wreck on the east coast. I wanted to do nothing but blame God for the sorrow He brought to me. I was living in that sorrow. And when I saw you, I was blaming God for what He did. But, as this is a small town, I know about what happened to your family. I know your mother died. I know you took the week off preaching and I know you came back the next week to your pulpit. And it seemed to me that you did not blame God because your mother died. I want you to know that since you don't blame God, I can't blame God either anymore!" The tears began to roll.

We took time that afternoon to explain how God loved Patti. And Patti confessed her faith in Christ and was baptized in my home church that evening, as our church did not have a baptistry. And after that, she trusted Christ in many ways and brought joy to many people.

I know that because Jesus died, I don't have to believe in a god who only wants to throw lightning bolts. I believe in a God who has a Son who cares for people. I believe in a God who wants to take my burdens and cares and share in my hurts and sorrows. I believe in a God who has opened the gates of heaven for those who love Him and serve Him and who will make that Son the Lord of their lives. I hope that as you go through life and face death that you will face it with the hope that takes away death's sting and prepares you for a home so grand the saints cannot even anticipate its beauty.

An Everyday Jesus for the Everyday Life – Conclusion
Making an Everyday Jesus Live Everyday In Our Lives
"A Parting Thought"

As I have found myself struggling with new challenges each day, and as I have tried to share with you some of the things that have stymied me, a new scripture has melted its way into my heart. You would probably say it is an old scripture, and you would be right. But in the course of these few moments we have had to spend together, this verse has become more alive to me. I feel it deserves your thought as well.

Psalm 23 is what some people call the Nightingale Psalm. James Gray, in his book "The Immigrant", says, "The nightingale always sings sweetest at the darkest hour."[8] I believe it is fair to say that about the 23rd Psalm. After all, Psalm 23 usually sings so sweetly when a loved one has passed from this life and we grieve. It shares its unique voice when we are struggling through difficult times. It is Psalm 23:4 that really helps us in darkness and despair: "Yea, though I walk through the valley of the shadow of death, I will fear no evil: for thou *art* with me; ..." (KJV)

Funny thing about shadows. Shadows are not real nor are shadows to be feared. I have yet to be injured by a shadow. I have never had a shadow stick out its foot and trip me. Never have I had a shadow grab me from behind and twist my arm.

Shadows are simply images that represent the real thing. A shadow of a tree is not a tree. The tree must be close by, but the shadow is not the tree.

In our quest to discover the Everyday Jesus for the Everyday Life, many of the valleys that we walk through are covered with shadows, but those shadows will not necessarily harm us. They might frighten us because of what they seem to represent. We readily admit that danger is close at hand, but the shadow is not the danger.

In this life, we realize that we will all, sometime, go through shadows of all of these daily situations. We daily might face the shadow of a fear, or the shadow of our family letting us down. The shadow of broken friendships might haunt us. The shadow of government intervention in our lives might loom over us. Difficult days of work and the concerns about failing finances may darken our steps. We might live in the gray fog of a marriage issue or even confusion from the mixed messages of morality we see in the world. Sickness may confound us and the prospect of death may pull us into uncertainty.

The truth is that other than death, we may not have to deal with many of the realities behind the shadows. It is not likely that each of these other nine concerns will come into our lives. To be sure, we will deal with some. However, the shadows will always be there used by the evil one to cause us to tremble and fail to trust in God!

Just as certainly as the Psalmist knew that God would be with him, we learn in the final words of Jesus to His disciples that there is a hope we can hold on to. Listen once again, please, to this part of Jesus' final directions to His disciples, ". . . and, lo, I am with you alway, *even* unto the end of the world. Amen." (Matthew 28:20b, KJV)

Are you afraid to take a step out of the house because bad things might happen or the future is uncertain? Do you wonder about the resolution to some problem that you are facing? Jesus is with you if you are His!

In John 12:18 we see that many of the people went to see Jesus because of the miracles that He did. I don't deny that this would be an astounding thing to see. It would attract me to Him, just as it did them.

But our premise throughout this time together has been, we don't need the miracles because Jesus Himself and His teachings are all we need. I hope I have been able to give you a reason to quit hoping for some miraculous answer to a problem and start looking at what the man Jesus said so that you can know a life that is not encumbered by fear but by living a life that is unique and trusting. I hope that I have reminded you that just as there was the care of God in David's dark valley that there is day to day care for you in your valleys when the shadows make you fear that some tragedy would befall you.

As a youngster, I used to love going to the department stores with my mom and dad when they would go shopping. I would explore. One time, when I was close to the ripe old age of 4, I wandered away from my mom on the second floor of a Montgomery Ward's store. I wanted to see what was in the inside of clothing displays. So, my nimble little feet led me inside a circular rack covered with ladies' blouses and dresses. I explored a minute and came out of the rack, unable to see my mom. I was terrified. I was alone. And I began to cry.

It only took my mom a few seconds to hear my cry, the mournful cry of being lost. She had only to step around the rack because she was on the other side. When I saw her my childish tears stopped and I knew that I had been found. I was saved. I thought it would take a miracle to find mom; it only took knowing a mother's heart.

Just as my mother heard my cries, I am confident that God will hear yours. There is no place you can go where He is not aware of your situation and His teachings cannot sustain you, even in the worst of times. That is the lesson learned from the Everyday Jesus for the Everyday Life. I hope that is what you are taking away from this book!

Reference Page:

[1] https://www.northernlightscentre.ca/northernlights.html

[2] http://www.bible-history.com/sketches/ancient/tax-collector.html

[3] **https://en.wikipedia.org/wiki/Sea_of_Galilee)(https://ferrelljenkins.wordpress.com/2009/12/12/a-little-storm-on-the-sea-of-galilee)**

[4] http://www.heartlight.org/articles/200704/20070427_friendship.html; 4/27/2007

[5] (Lincoln's Last Days by Bill O'Reilly; Henry Holt and Company, New York, New York, (c) 2012 by Bill O'Reilly

[6] (https://www.conference-board.org/publications/publicationdetail.cfm?publicationid=2785&centerId=4

[7] (Ketuboth 7:6 cited in paper by https://www.wisereaction.org/ebooks/wenham_divorce_first.pdf - Paper presented in Northern Ireland)

[8] (winsome-words.tumblr.com)

About the Author

Randy Whitehead shares a birthday with former President Dwight David Eisenhower, October 14. Of course, Ike had a few years on him. But he treasured the signed card that came from the former chief executive, to commemorate that common day.

Married to his beautiful wife Lois in 1974, he has been in ministry since October 15, 1972. He and Lois are the parents of two wonderful daughters and he and Lois enjoy a great relationship with their sons-in-law (at least they think they do). Also, with 12 grandkids, they love spoiling each of them.

Having spent 46 years in church ministry, Randy has accumulated a lot of knowledge, and a lot of stories. He is also a singer/song writer and has about 50 songs to his credit. He loves serving the Lord in creative ways and trusts this book continues the process.

What life holds for Randy, only God knows. But he appreciates all the special friends God has put in his way, trusting that the Lord turns each opportunity to visit into a chance to change lives in a real way as many he has visited with have changed his in marvelous and wonderful ways. Randy would love to hear how stories and studies in this book have changed your life. Contact him at **randallwwhitehead@yahoo.com**!

This book would not be the same with out the tireless effort his wife Lois played in helping read and proofread for grammar and wording. Her hard work is so appreciated!

Made in the USA
Columbia, SC
18 August 2018